GRACE, GRIT AND GLORY

Grace, Grit and Glory

ALEX & PEGGY BUCHANAN

KINGSWAY PUBLICATIONS
EASTBOURNE

Unless otherwise indicated, biblical quotations are from the
New American Standard Bible © The Lockman Foundation,
1960, 1962, 1963, 1968, 1971, 1972, 1973.

The poems by Hannah Hurnard first appeared in
Mountains of Spices (Kingsway Publications).

ISBN 0 86065 721 3

Printed in Great Britain for
KINGSWAY PUBLICATIONS LTD
1 St Anne's Road, Eastbourne, E Sussex BN21 3UN by
BPCC Hazells Ltd, Aylesbury, Bucks
Typeset by J&L Composition Ltd, Filey, North Yorkshire

Contents

Foreword

When I first heard that the Buchanan family were writing their autobiography, I suggested the title 'God is Not Handicapped'. The one who changed water into wine can transform liabilities into assets. The reader will be compelled to ask and answer the question: Has the unique ministry of Alex and Peggy been exercised in spite of, or because of, their severe handicaps?

This book is unlikely to be a bestseller. For one thing, it will mean most to those who have met or known them 'in the flesh' (a phrase that carries a peculiar poignancy in their case). All those who have benefited from their ministry and friendship will be fascinated to learn how they became what they are.

But readers hoping for sensational success or comforting consolation will be disappointed. They will find here a ruthless honesty in describing both the outward struggle with physical problems, and the inward struggle with mental doubts and emotional fears. Those who naively think that spiritual victories are easy or instant may well be disillusioned; those whose battle has been long and hard will be encouraged to 'bash on' (one of Alex's favourite exhortations, to himself as well as to others).

There is a doctrine called 'the perseverance of the

saints'. But does this mean saints are destined to persevere (as the Calvinist would say) or determined to persevere (as the Arminian would say)? Is it divine grace or human guts that enables St Alex and St Peggy to overcome? I believe the answer is both. The Lord is able to keep from falling those who keep themselves in his love (Jude 21–24).

One thing is certain—heaven (and the new earth) will be inhabited by 'overcomers'. They will receive compensation for their sufferings and rewards for their faithfulness. I can't wait to see Alex and Peggy in their new bodies—she skipping and dancing all over the place while he grins from ear to ear!

Which brings me to their humour, which like their honesty seasons their tale with salt. Laughter and tears are never far apart; but they have chosen to laugh at themselves rather than cry for themselves. That is why their souls are not crippled with self-pity. The humour is simple, born out of suffering. The book might well have been sub-titled 'The progress of a pilgrim's bunion'!

Many are puzzled by this unique combination of earthy realism and heavenly anticipation. A conversation can switch from cars and computers to judgement and glory without a break—or even a warning! Not a few have been unnerved by talking with someone to whom the next world is as real, even more real, than this one.

Some have been afraid of Alex, but that is because they know he is not afraid to tell them the truth as the Lord has shown it to him. It is the fear of being exposed. Even Peggy's penetrating gaze can make one feel that nothing can be hidden! In their different ways they are both fearless—of people. That is because they both fear God, which is the foundation of their wisdom.

Only eternity will reveal how many lives they have influenced for good. I found the most moving part of this book to be the tributes from the three children, who wanted to have their say. In a different way, they also have 'lived with' severe handicaps, yet the Lord has clearly used this to enrich and mature them.

Those who would emulate, or even envy, the prophetic and pastoral ministry exercised by this unique couple will be sobered by this account of the way the Lord has dealt with them. Who would choose to go through what they have been through? Of course, even they did not choose to. But they did choose to let the Lord use it all for his glory. And he has done so.

David J. D. Pawson

Preface
Hallelujah—Ouch!

How does someone cope with the frustration of not being healed, yet still sustain a demanding ministry? Many years ago at Castlerigg Camp, I was asked to give my testimony in two words; it came to me in these: 'Hallelujah—Ouch!'

If Peggy had written the book alone she would have called it *He Only Married me for my Mobility Allowance*. Obviously this is not true! I did not marry Peggy for her pensions!

While this book does not refer to everything that has happened to us, we want it to say something helpful to the frustrated, and to underline Bible principles more than to tell the Buchanan story. The book is not particularly about faith, nor is it primarily about healing, nor is it about a tragedy. It is an account of how two ordinary people battled with the frustration of not being healed, while still having to sustain a ministry. Sickness and its attendant problems have tried us severely for many years, but this book recounts the way in which God enabled us to cope with this difficult situation while still fulfilling the ministry he has given us. We have received much grace; this has been mingled with our human grit; and the result has been that we have been able to give him glory. This is not a boast, but a testimony.

Because there are people who have had far more difficult things to cope with, and who have probably triumphed more gloriously than we have, we do not want to be melodramatic in this account. Our story pales into insignificance beside many we have read, and it made us hesitate before writing, but we have been urged to write it, so we have done so.

Our reason for writing is simply to encourage those who are sick, frustrated and disabled to press on, and to stick to their belief that God *is* good, whatever circumstances might seem to say: to encourage them to live in the light of eternity so that suffering is seen from a better perspective. To encourage the sick to lay up treasure in heaven rather than to spend our days down here in gloom and spiritual inactivity. However sick we are, God can and will use us, if we want him to do so. Don't ask us to unravel the mystery of suffering; we can't. But we have learned to make sickness work for us. None of us likes pain, but if we are stuck with it, then let us make it productive pain. If pain is a bully who would master us, let us turn the tables on it and make it work for us instead. We are learning with Paul to say that 'the sufferings of this present time are not worthy to be compared with the glory which will follow' (Rom 8:18). It is better to be a hero in heaven than a misery on the earth. Our credentials for writing this book are passable but not spectacular.

The facts are these. Peggy has suffered from MS for twenty-five years, with its attendant pain, sleeplessness, discomfort, lack of mobility, and frustration. She was a very active, outgoing, adventurous, energetic woman. The frustration of comparative immobility has therefore been one of her keenest trials. The travelling ministry which God gave us has brought to her the problems of new and changing lodgings, some with difficult toilets and all with different bedrooms. A gluten-free diet is an added complication sometimes, and the continual embarrassment of having to be lifted and carried on occasions irks her too. She has had endless tests, injections, pills, physiotherapy, osteopathy, oxygen treatment, diets, and vitamins. Doctors have grilled her, Christians have ministered to her by anointing her with oil, giving her prophecies, prayers, and exortations. But she is still disabled.

I too have suffered during a period of forty-five years—from various things such as spinal curvature, a fractured skull, meningitis, radical mastoid, per-forated ear drums, acute facial pain and paralysis, Bells palsy, and teenage acne! I have had many operations to remedy damage done when a scalpel slipped and severed a vital nerve. The resulting repairs caused many complications and brought me close to death more than once.

We have sought God diligently for healing; we have fasted, prayed, agonised, attended healing meetings, listened to testimonies, read all the books, bared our souls before God and his people in case sin was preventing our healing. But we are not healed yet, though we have been abundantly blessed spiritually.

Jim Graham, a dear and precious friend of ours, said after fervent prayer for us, 'Alex, the only answer I have for you is the sheer sovereignty of God. I cannot find any other, however earnestly I seek it.' I believed him, although this does not cause us to relinquish our quest. Nor does Jim for one minute suggest that we do, for God has never told us to quit praying for the manifestation of his power in healing. If he does tell us to stop, we will, but until he does we will *never* quit. We have seen others healed after we have prayed for them, some quite miraculously, so we need no convincing that God does heal. It heightens the mystery, but it does not paralyse our activity.

Our children deserve credit for the way they coped with sick parents, and their honest comments form a part of this book. Many good friends have prayed for us through the years, and we shall look forward to their being rewarded in heaven for doing so. Above all—and it's worth saying again—God has given us grace to mix with our grit so that we have been able to bring him glory.

Alex and Peggy Buchanan. York 1992

1

God's Unlikely Choice

God loaned me life, and took a risk.
He gave me choice, and waited long.
He stayed his hand, and spared my life,
Till I could see that I was wrong.

He saw his Son, and looked at me.
My shoddy state enabled him —
To show his grace, remaking me —
Into the likeness of his Son.

Your courage, Lord, amazes me.
Such mighty grace, so full and free.
I choose to bow, and own you, Lord;
To live according to your Word.

A.B.

If God does take risks, then they are wonderfully
calculated risks. Perhaps they were calculated way
back in the council chamber of eternity, before
creation began.

Peggy and I are so glad that God saw us among the
millions of the 'weak and foolish . . .' (1 Cor 1:27) and
took a risk, and chose us to become his 'children and

heirs. . .' (Rom 8:17). We are in good company: Gladys
Aylward, a humble housemaid who led many Chinese
to God; Mary Jones, a poor Welsh girl whose persistence led to the Bible Society being formed . . . and
so many others.

In Bible times too, God took risks with unlikely
people. Judas: the treacherous, thieving disciple who
would not have been allowed within a mile of the
offering box in today's churches, yet Jesus chose him,
gave him every chance, and loved him as well as the
rest. Thomas: who would have been eased out by many
church leaders today, in case he lowered the church's
morale through his doubts and fears, yet Jesus elicited
pure worship from him when later Thomas said, 'My
Lord, and my God.' Gideon was not too promising as a
mighty man of valour, cowering in the silo. (He
reminds me of our youngest son who, when a little boy
and over-powered by his bigger brother, said 'Daddy,
get him off me before I kill him.') Yet God saw Gideon
from a different perspective, and chose him to save a
nation. It has been said that if God had courage
enough to use Balaam's ass, then he can use anyone.
Peggy and I claim to be as eligible as the ass!

I wonder if God has fun choosing his servants. Has
he got a glorious twinkle in his eye as he sets apart his
ambassadors in full view of astounded angels? The
Bible says that the angels long to look into the things
which God does among his people (1 Pet 1:12). They
must be fascinated! I have read all the commentaries to
find out more about God's choice of man, but they are
as puzzled as I am. So, the best thing is to accept
Scripture which describes us as those whom God has
'made . . . a kingdom [a royal race] priests to God' (Rev
1:6), and get on with our training as priestly kings and
queens.

It is interesting that God chose me from the Brethren, and Peggy from the Anglicans. It proves to me that God is not denominational. He is not destroying our denominations; instead, he is invading them!

Two people, one flesh

I was born in 1928 in Willesden near London. My parents were quite poor, although my father worked hard in the building trade, and in anything else he could find, but with little financial reward. I remember him cycling for many miles to one of his jobs, and he always arrived home exhausted. We were reasonably happy, although often rather hungry. More than once our diet was augmented with cheap scraps of meat, which my sister and I collected in an old pram from a store a mile away. Mum was constantly tired and ill, so my older sister Betty and I had quite a bit to do. Neither of us was dressed in the latest fashion, and the other children at school often pointed this out; but at least we were clothed, praise God.

Mum and Dad were Christians, though Mum had the stronger faith. Because of their Christianity, Betty and I were brought up with some knowledge of God, and my mother taught me to read when I was very young. She taught us from the Bible, and this helped us later on to find God for ourselves, for Betty loves the Lord, too.

I was often ill with ear trouble, and other ailments, and this curtailed my schooling quite frequently. The fact that it was wartime did not help either. Even when we did get to school, we had to run repeatedly to the air raid shelters – where education was very secondary! However, I became a voracious reader, and I devoured dictionaries (not literally, I was never *that* hungry). Higher education was denied me, and this led to some resentment in my heart later when many of my friends went on to university. But God needs people in all walks of life, and he does not make mistakes.

Working life

My first job, at the age of fourteen, was to hang on to a chain in the back of a parcels lorry, and to help the driver to deliver them all over North London. This gave me a real instinct for survival! A year later I began to work in the GEC electrical factory in Wembley. At the age of seventeen I moved to a garage and became a car mechanic. The next few years saw me briefly working in a machine shop, then in an organ-building works with a linked building firm. The organ-building work involved me in long-distance truck driving. After all this, I went to Bible College at the age of twenty-six for a year in 1954; and then, when I could not go to Ethiopia as a missionary, I worked as a crisp salesman (failed), and finally in a laboratory.

At the time it seemed like being a jack of all trades and master of none. In fact, unguessed by me, it was all a part of my training for Christian work – although I admit that the syllabus does not closely resemble that in the average Bible College! Truck driving was a training in evangelism; the hitchhikers whom I picked up used to listen to me preaching the gospel as we lumbered along. (They only had one other alternative.) Working in filthy factories enabled me later on to witness to Liverpool dockers, for they understood blisters and piecework as I did.

When I was fifteen-and-a-half, I had an accident in which I unknowingly fractured my skull. This eventually brought on cerebral meningitis, a radical mastoid, high temperature, and a few other unpleasant things. I was rushed into hospital and became comatose. During one of my brief spells of consciousness, the surgeons told me that I had only a short time to live. This did not make me radiantly happy. In fact it terrified me. I knew that God existed, and that he was holy, and I was not. I cried out for mercy saying 'Lord, spare my life, and I will give it back to you.' Thankfully, I can say he did. (I *am* alive, honestly.)

It was at this time that I saw my first vision. I saw the gates of heaven, which seemed to be made of solid light. (How else can you describe them?) I felt myself drawn to and through them, and I knew that this was death. Then I heard the voice of God saying to me, 'Not yet, *my child*—a little more rough tossing.' (I was not a Christian at this time, which shows the grace and foreknowledge of God in that he called me his child.) I felt drawn back from death, and, according to the doctors, began to recover from that moment.

Encounter with God

After recovery, I went back with my ungodly friends, but I discovered that God is remarkably determined when he sets his sights on men and decides to draw them to himself. He heard my promise, and now he had come to claim me. I grew desperate, and God had courage enough to allow that, knowing I would respond eventually. I considered suicide but had not the courage to do it. The Holy Spirit, who always works hand in hand with the Father and the Son, reminded me of the gospel hall where my sister and I had gone as children; so I went back to Glebe Hall in Kenton, and I heard the gospel again. Some weeks

later, around my eighteenth birthday, I turned to
God and found him waiting for me.

I did not grow very quickly as a Christian, largely
because of physical handicap, and embarrassment. I
had considerable surgery, with interesting results,
including paralysis, deafness, a spot of blindness, and
much pain. Consequently, I shrank from people,
even in the church, for I could not hear, and I looked
fairly grotesque. Then one of the elders' wives took
pity on me and began to pass me notes of the sermons
so that I could at least get something from the
meetings. This gave me a little confidence, and I felt
to some degree part of things.

In his mercy, God put some godly men and women
in my way, to whom I refer in my book *Bible Meditation, Prayer and Prophecy*. I shall always thank God
for them, because they never let go of me, and they
steered me towards the Lord. Their homes were
havens to me, and it was in them that I was first made
to study the Bible in depth.

Hunger for God

While all this was going on, I began to feel a deep
longing to know God better than I did, and to serve
him in his church. Predictably the Enemy worked on
my deep-seated inferiority, convincing me that I was
no use, and a wreck into the bargain. After hearing
the elders pray and preach, and comparing my sparse
knowledge of the Bible and clumsy private prayers
with theirs, I agreed with him and descended into
despair. But God did not give up on me!

After a while I had a great desire to pray in public.
Week after week I tried and failed. But on one
famous night I made my attempt. It was a total
disaster. Being very deaf, but thinking that there was

a silence, I shot to my feet to pray. What I did not know was that there was a girl behind me resting her feet on the rungs of my chair, with her elbows on her knees. Consequently, when I stood up, she collapsed in a heap, bringing chairs and people with her onto the floor. Looking with horror at this scene, I fled, not to return for many weeks. Eventually, with the elders' help I did it: I prayed! This fiasco helped me in later years when God gave me the leadership of a national prayer movement, to encourage many other timid people to open their mouths and pray. How typical of God to use a man as deaf as a post, with his wife who cannot walk, to travel all over the world raising up prayer meetings!

God fanned the flames of my desire for him. He put into my hands books about Murray McCheyne, Jonathan Edwards, Charles Finney, John Hyde, Andrew Murray, and the like. These men became my mentors, and they set my heart aflame for holy things. I asked God to let me do something for him, and he did. At one of the churches I attended they asked for someone to clean the church toilets, and God asked me if I would do it. At first, comparing the toilet with the pulpit, I wondered if the Almighty had got his guidance wrong, but eventually I did it as an act of obedience. So began my ministry unto the Lord!

Urged on by God

I eventually settled at Deane Avenue Evangelical Church in Ruislip, Middlesex, where God gave me grace to venture into Sunday school work. It was difficult when the children made fun of my facial deformity, but it was encouraging when some of them found Jesus as their Saviour, especially because some of

them are following the Lord to this day. Covenanter
work followed, and boys' camps, all of which proved
extremely fruitful. But I felt a deep dissatisfaction
every time I read the book of Acts and compared the
work of the disciples with mine. For a while I almost
hated the Scriptures because they showed me up in
such a bad light. I used to fast and pray, sometimes all
night, but that did not seem to make much difference. I would scream out to God, saying, 'How
much more do I have to do to qualify for your power?'
Then I would dissolve into tears in case I had hurt
God by my rudeness. But I underestimated his love
and patience; he led me on and did not condemn me.

I also found him determined to care for me by
leading me into even more stretching things. For
example, the church held open-air meetings to which
we were all expected to go, and in which we were
expected to participate. I resisted this because I was
so self-conscious, and felt that it was not my work
anyway. Some weeks later I did go with them to Chalk
Farm in London. We set up our ancient amplifier by a
bus stop opposite an advertising hoarding. We young
people were then asked to come to the microphone
one by one to shout our 'gospel bullets' – ie, a text
from the Bible. Several did so, without anyone being
'hit' by them. I was dragged from behind the bus
shelter where I had taken refuge, and shoved up to
the microphone. My mind went completely blank. In
a flat panic, I found myself looking at the adver-
tisement opposite, and I bawled out the words on it
saying 'What we want is Watneys' (ale).

I have never before seen elders in glorious Techni-
color as I did then. They went white, red, purple in
their amazement and disapproval. Hastening to make
amends, I bleated over the amplifier 'No, friends,

what I meant was "What we want is Jesus."' But alas, the spirit went out of the meeting, and we all went home. Nobody said much on the train home! But God persisted with me, and I found myself dragged out again in the open air by dear Len Tayler, who had a voice like a musical foghorn. He chose a spot on a traffic roundabout on the main A40 by Northolt Airport, reasoning that if we could reach people there, we could reach them anywhere. He was right; we did; namely the police in their patrol car. We gave them a tract, plus the name and addresses which they asked for, and then they kindly and firmly gave us a nice ride home! No souls, no voice left, but more experience. God in his wisdom pushed me into more and more of these embarrassing experiences; he allowed more failures too, but also some encouragements.

It was during this period, when I was twenty, that I worked for an organ-building firm, and God reminded me that many of my workmates were heading for hell. He asked me what I was doing about it, and I could only answer, 'Nothing, really, Lord; you know how shy I am.' But how does anyone evade God? So eventually in a feeble effort to do something, I went into the toilet and scrawled John 3:16 on the wall, and got out quick. Our foreman went in shortly afterwards; after some meditation, he saw the verse, received it, and was born again. There are other ways of winning souls, but the main point of this story is that it illustrates the grace, patience, and perseverance of a lovingly determined God. He was saying that my future work depended on perseverance and training at the time. I love him for it, now! Evangelism is not a pious dream; it is a required reality.

Practical Christianity

The fellowship was building a new church at this
time, and, because I was in the building trade, I drove
lorries, stacked bricks, repaired machinery, and had
charge of the stores. It was in the stores that I first
found out the men's favourite motto, which was 'The
Lord helps those who help themselves!' My boss,
whom I had led to the Lord by now, gave me carte
blanche to use any of our equipment to help build the
new church. So we did.

There followed some miraculous answers to
prayer, which built up my faith greatly. At the time,
building materials were almost impossible to obtain
because of the war's aftermath. We needed a round
window for the front gable of the new church, so we
prayed for one. Going in to work the following day, I
found that the manager wanted me to shift a huge
pile of rubbish in the yard. This annoyed me greatly,
for I reckoned that I was not a mere labourer!
However, I started shifting it. There were beams of
wood, old bricks, lumps of concrete, corrugated iron
sheets and the like. There must have been twenty tons
of this stuff, and it took me all day to sort it out. By
about 5pm I had got to the bottom of the pile, and
there in front of my eyes was one round window,
complete with coloured glass, and not one piece
broken! I rushed up to the office and asked my boss if
we could buy it, and he said, 'Go on, take the ***
thing, I don't want it.' It is in the front of Deane
Avenue Evangelical Church, South Ruislip, to this
day.

On another occasion we needed some special bricks
which again were unobtainable. The day after we
prayed for them I was sent to a Roman Catholic
convent in Sussex with some materials. As I was

driving out after delivering them, a nun ran after me saying, 'Excuse me, are you the lorry driver?' Rather nonplussed at this lack of observation, I said 'Yes.' She then said, 'I beseech you in the name of our Lady to take away that pile of rubbish by the gate.' How could I refuse? So I shovelled this pile into my lorry, and after a while I became aware of a thump every time I threw a shovelful into the truck. Investigation showed me that I was loading bricks with the muck. They were special bricks; the type we had prayed for the night before. To cut a story short, they are in the foundations today; laid in the name of our Father!

Other things followed; 'unobtainable' steel beams being given to us; windows being made for us by a nearby factory by permission of the wartime authorities. Truly our faith grew because of our needs and difficulties. We had a lot of fun building the place, although it had its moments. I found attempting to stand on a high trestle and make plaster stick on a wall was hard enough; doing so alongside an accomplished plasterer was harder still, especially as my batch of plaster seemed to be quite unconverted, and definitely 'non-stick'. But to talk about the Second Coming and heaven and the Lord under such conditions not only kept my temper in check, but taught me much of what I know today. Prayer meetings round a roaring fire in an old oil drum were very special, too.

Moving on

Right in the middle of all this work, when I could least be spared, God called me to Matlock Bible College (now Moorlands). I could not believe it; neither could the elders. For a start, I was a key man in the building

operations; secondly, I was the most unsuitable candi-
date for full-time work: uneducated, not very bright,
and far from able in public ministry. I told God all
this, but he seemed quite unworried. Then I told the
elders, who were extremely worried, and wholeheartedly agreed with my verdict that I was not good
enough. But, again, God was so gracious; he confirmed in a dream, and again in a vision, that he was
indeed calling me to go to Bible College. So I went. It
was there that I was to meet Peggy.

Peggy had been born in 1934 at Buxton in
Derbyshire. Her father was a skilled engineer from
Darlington, and her mother a countrywoman from
Masham in Yorkshire. The home was a loving one,
and with her brother Gordon, Peggy experienced no
great traumas in her youth. (In fact, as Kevin
and Sue Jarrett said when they read the manu-
script for this book, she seems quite normal in comparison with me!) Her mother had been converted
through the ministry of Gypsy Smith when she was
fourteen. She was an ardent chapel goer in Masham,
and followed the Lord sincerely. While out for a bike
ride one day, she met Jim Sutherland, whom she
eventually married, and soon became happily
immersed in home and family. At that time Peggy's
father was not a Christian, but many years later he
became a keen Christian and is a great example to
others in the church even though he is now eighty-
nine. He uses his home for prayer meetings, and is
greatly loved. It shows that with God, it is never too
late to be saved if people are willing to find and obey
him.

At the start of the war, Peggy's father, who was an
engineer, applied for two jobs, one in Cumbria and
the other in Manchester. Because he applied first to

Manchester, he was required by the authorities to take that one. In actual fact, God was directing operations because there was a good Anglican church in Cheadle, where they settled.

The Anglican curate contacted them, and persevered in spite of Peggy's mother, who insisted to him that she was 'completely satisfied with her home and family, thank you'. Peggy and her brother went to the Sunday school at this church, and, later on, to the gospel meetings. Peggy was always uneasy on Advent Sunday, when the Coming of Jesus was preached. She had privately asked him into her heart on several occasions, and had a mental understanding of the gospel. A favourite hymn was 'My hope is built on nothing less than Jesus' blood and righteousness', but her faith was all rather cerebral and unreal. On her seventeenth birthday she attended a church Crusade service, and stayed behind for counsel. Someone showed her John 1:12: 'To as many as received him, to them he gave the right to become the children of God', and she was converted. The next day, facing up to the verse 'You are not your own, you are bought with a price—1 Cor 6:19', she set about the surrender aspect of her Christian pilgrimage, though God, in his grace, had already been working on her heart for a long time.

After leaving Moseley Hall Grammar School Peggy worked in Manchester as a tax clerk (TC3, the lowest grade), and learned a lot about people. (You do when you help business men who are old enough to be your father to fill in their tax forms!)

Growing slowly as a Christian, ever eager to get it right, she would go out at every and any appeal. The scripture 'Christ died for the ungodly' became precious; in fact it came as a real revelation – a 'now' word from God—because she had previously believed that he died only for nice people. God made sure that godly people met her at this time. One of the more mature young people, Evelyn Brown, taught her much about God, and also introduced her to the British Jews Society. To this day, Peggy has a deep love for the Jews and later, after our marriage, we had the joy of preaching in Israel many many times.

The Sunday school superintendent in her home church in Cheadle (St Phillip's) urged her on in Bible study and introduced her to the healthy practice of 'praying round' the circle. During the harvest guest service the young people would gather in another room to pray while the vicar preached, and this brought some to Christ. As part of her service to the Lord, Peggy used to collect a little boy and take him to Sunday school, but one day his mother announced that he would not come any more because they had joined the Jehovah's Witnesses. This grieved her, and it urged her and others to pray even harder. Prayer ceased to be a duty, and took on deeper meaning for her; even in those early days of Christian life, God was teaching Peggy about intercession, and she has been a sensitive and tender-hearted intercessor ever since. This was good training for the times when her husband led a nationwide prayer movement. How wise God is! The godly Sunday school superintendent, the deaconess, the youth leader and the curate were all used by God to help her by example, teaching, and encouragement, too. How we both thank God for them now.

God caused one of the young people to introduce a hymn during a meeting, and it has stuck with Peggy ever since. It encapsulates her heart's desire – Charles

Vincent's hymn 'Oh the bitter shame and sorrow . . .', with its lovely progression, 'all of self, and none of Thee . . . Some of self, and some of Thee . . . Less of self, and more of Thee . . . None of self, and all of Thee'.

After a while, Peggy became uneasy, feeling that she had wrongly abandoned her desire to be a teacher. Looking back now, she sees clearly that God had known her desire to get closer to him, and to do something more with her life; he was taking her into a new era in which she would learn the lessons that would enable her to go through the rigorous times of sickness and disability which were to begin when she was thirty years old. Mercifully, she did not know that she would lose all the freedom of her young womanhood because of this crippling disease.

This was only a beginning, and after much thought she decided that teaching was indeed part of God's plan for her life, so she applied to a teacher training college in Matlock, and was accepted there in 1954.

2

God's Careful Guidance

Thy gentleness hath made me great,
And I would gentle be.
'Tis Love that plans my lot, not Fate,
Lord, teach this grace to me.
When gales and storms Thy love doth send
That I with joy may meekly bend.

Thy servants must not strive nor fight,
But as their Master be,
'Tis meekness wins, not force nor might,
Lord, teach this grace to me.
Though others should resist my love,
I may be gentle as a dove.

Hannah Hurnard

Guidance is rarely permanent; it comes in stages. God generally moves us from one thing to another (although I am not suggesting that when God guides us to our partners in marriage we should take that as temporary guidance!). Our experiences in Matlock

were another stage for me and Peggy in our
pilgrimage.

God created man with a need to be directed. He
never envisaged him as a self-sufficient, independent
creature, but one who would look to his Creator for
direction. It was this need which would ensure close
fellowship between God and humanity. The desire
to be self-sufficient and independent was the very
thing which brought about Satan's downfall, and he
in turn brought about the downfall of humanity.
Humanism is an example of this attitude. The
humanists say, 'I will guide my own course. I will be
my own god. I am capable of fulfilling and controlling
my own destiny. I need no outside help from God or
anyone else.'

But God was ready for all these complications. In
fact he saw them as opportunities to show himself
strong on behalf of all who would be willing to abide
by his will.

He sees things very clearly; he has been right to the
end of history and back again. Of course he knows
the way. Can there be a better guide?

The words 'drawing' and 'guiding' are twins. God
draws us towards salvation so that he can guide us
into it. In my case he guided me first towards, and
then away from the gates of death. God guided me
away from the girls I might have chosen and put me
on course to the one girl I have ever truly loved. In
this way, he enabled me to fulfil my work. He guided
me away from further education—it is so right and
vital for others, but it was not God's plan for me. He
guided me into poverty before I went to college. It
was all part of his training in faith. He does not call
everyone to sell everything, but he did call me to do
so.

The school of experience

I left Ruislip in 1954 to go to Matlock Bible College. Sadly no one commended me to it from Deane Avenue; neither was there any support forthcoming. But it was necessary to learn the lesson that if God calls, we must obey God rather than men. We must also learn to trust that if God calls us, then he is responsible for the bills.

God required me to sell nearly everything I had, so I arrived at college with the clothes I stood up in, my Bible, a bike, and *Young's Concordance* (which also doubled as a tie press). No student grants were available then, at least not to me. Thank God for that! I would never have learned much about faith if I had had a substantial grant.

Many and varied were the ways in which God met financial needs. One such was when I needed dental treatment. The dentist was an atheist. When it was finished, he said that he would send his bill in a few days. I gulped, and said that would be fine. He realised that I would not be exactly flush with money, so he sneered at my college badge, and said in front of all his staff, 'Your loving heavenly Father going to pay your bill, is he?' His bill arrived the next day; it was for £3.10s.

I spread this before God, together with the verse Philippians 4:13—'My God shall supply all your need', and the contents of my pockets, which consisted of an old halfpenny. I prayed that God would vindicate his word in front of the dentist and all his staff. The next day I received a letter from Tipton where I had never been, and knew no one. It contained £3.10s! I enjoyed explaining these events to a startled dentist, plus all his staff. I still have the letter—and the fillings.

My purpose in writing these things is to pay tribute
to the grace of God in allowing me to experience not
only much need, but his loving provision to meet it.
My whole course at MBC was characterised by the
grace of God. There were inches of rust on my
brains; I could still scarcely hear; and I had no real
answer for those who said, 'Where are you going as a
missionary when you finsih?' All I knew was that God
had said 'go'.

We learned much in the lectures: original Greek
came into them somewhere, but mine was highly
original Greek! To be honest, I learned far more with
my heart than I ever did with my head. God helped
my prayer life by causing me to be chosen to light the
college boiler.

This was one of the most stubborn, unconverted
bits of scrap I have ever seen. Lighting it required
wood, matches, dynamite, sweat, toil, tears and a
miracle. I had to be up at dawn to do it, though
medically I was supposed to need ten hours' sleep a
night. How gracious God is to demolish our fleshly
myths. By the time the blessed boiler was happily
aglow, it was not worth going back to bed, so I got into
the habit of going up to the one small tree on the top
of Oaker Hill, and kneeling down under it to pray.
The whole of Matlock was visible from there, and it
was from that time that I began to seek God on behalf
of whole towns, and larger projects.

As the course went on, I became burdened for
Ethiopia, and began to pray earnestly for that land.
In fact it became the focus of my intense desire to
serve the Lord. I had every intention of going there
as a missionary. But, again, God intervened, this time
causing a doctor to confirm that my health would
never stand it. God often gives us a focus as he guides

our lives. He keeps us heading that way, then at the
end he says, 'Turn left. Here is another focus.' I
suppose this highlights the fact that he is far more
interested in what we become than he is in what we
do. But all the time he guides us if we are willing to be
guided. Whether we are guided or not is seen mostly
in our obedience.

Some while after I started at the college, my quiet
times dried up completely. Prayer was dead, the Bible
untouched. I took to the hills to find out why. I could
only cry out, 'What has gone wrong, Lord?' After
several days the Holy Spirit convinced me that my
offering of my hopes of marriage to God was an
incomplete offering. I *thought* I had been sincere, and
that I had surrendered my hopes completely but in
fact I was still secretly clinging to that hope. I had not
truly given it up. There followed one of the most
agonising battles I have ever fought in my life, but it
ended in a true sacrifice of my hopes this time.
Shortly afterwards I met Peggy Sutherland, who is
now my beloved wife.

We were a varied bunch at college. Many were
Brethren; a few were Pentecostal; and a sprinkling
were Baptists. Some of the students were interested in
divine healing, and others talked about an experience
of second blessing. Holiness was popular, at least in
theory. The doctrine of predestination led most of us
to the brink of insanity, but much talk about the
students at the girls' training college nearby 'saved'
us. I eventually plucked up courage to ask one of the
lecturers if he believed in divine healing, but he
didn't. Being extremely unwell at the time, I asked
some of the students if they would pray for my
healing; they did so with great enthusiasm.

They decided that anointing with oil was vital, but

their version of holy anointing oil was actually made
by Esso Petroleum—for cars! It did nothing at all for
my healing, nor would the local barber touch me for
weeks. It did not bless me, nor was I healed. However
a hunger to know God better, and to see more of his
power, had arisen in many of the students. They
longed for things similar to those seen by the early
disciples, including the healing of the sick. There was
a measure of blessing in my own preaching around
the local chapels, but all the time I was crying out in
my heart for more of the great power of God. I felt
that I would rather die if my present experience was
all that I would see of his blessing.

God brings us together

I had always wanted to be married and have a wife
and children of my own; and as I said before, there
were several Christian girls to whom I was attracted.
Few of them reciprocated! Neither different tooth-
paste nor a fresh hair style did anything for my
marital ambitions! Seriously though, their lack of
response increased my feeling of uselessness and
heightened a sense of rejection. Yet God was using
this struggle to make me decide whom I wanted most,
a wife or God. After several days and nights of
waiting on God, I finally said, 'Lord Jesus, it is you I
want more than anyone else. Please take my desire for
a wife and family, and either keep it and I will stay
single, or give me my desire in your own time.' This
prayer of surrender gave me peace and enabled me
to set out to serve God as a single man.

While I was living through all these things, God was
dealing with a girl named Peggy Sutherland. She had
left Cheadle, and was now a student at the nearby

Matlock Teacher Training College. Like me, she had
discovered that the Matlock Brethren Assembly was a
live church, and something of a gathering place for
students from both colleges. Having very little
money, she could not afford the bus fare to the
evangelical Anglican church several miles away, so
she came to the Brethren. However the real reason
for her attendance was because the Sunday school
superintendent had asked her to teach the children
there. Convinced that it was right to teach there, she
felt it logical to attend there, too.

We both learned so much through the Assembly
teaching, and although things like tithing were
familiar to me, they were new to Peggy. One shilling
(5p) out of her weekly ten shillings went to the Lord.
(She has received much more than 50p a week since
then!) Our lifelong habit has since been to regard a
tenth as belonging to God. This is a good start but has
one danger; actually all our money belongs to God.
Some people give nine tenths and live off the rest.
Peggy says, 'I don't think I could have lived off 5p
then, but God knew at what stage I was in my
pilgrimage then. How gracious he is.' Other significant lessons for her were that she learned to honour
the Bible as the word of God, not just as a book of
sermons.

Yet another result of the teaching there was that
she was challenged about water baptism at this
stage, and, after prayer and instruction, she was
baptised in Clumber Hall in Nottingham. The elder
from Matlock who baptised her used the pet name
Peggy, by which she had been called from her earliest
years, as well as her real name, Flora Ursula. He
called her 'Flora Ursula Peggy', doing a thorough job.
As we mature, many of us would like to be baptised

again now that we see its deeper meaning. For Peggy
at that time, it was a step of obedience, and she has
only realised the full implications as she has grown in
Christ. But God understands and appreciates what is
in our hearts at any given time.

Another blessing from that time was that she
learned to trust God more than people. She says,
'Alex Buchanan was, and is, a strong spiritual man,
but I had to learn not to trust in his spirituality at the
cost of trusting God for myself, and seeking him for
myself. A version of a hymn helped me: "I dare not
trust the sweetest frame (even Alex's), but wholly lean
on Jesus Name." There is a fine balance to be kept in
this matter. In later years, after we were married and
had a home and children to look after, it was
sometimes easier and possibly right to let Alex pray
through the major matters such as the choice of the
children's schools. Other matters, such as our
eventual move to York, we prayed through together.'

The Brethren Assembly gathered at that time (in
1954) in the St John's Ambulance hut in Matlock.
Prayer was made there, as well as the chinchilla rabbit
show. Both had an effect on the place! The gospel
was preached there, and the Real Ale Society prac-
tised there. At first, Peggy and I were simply friends;
no one else believed it, but it was true. She was a
lovely, fresh-faced girl, a little naive, not too mature
as a Christian, but lovely. She was the president of the
college CU, and very popular with the students. She
had a great desire to win students for Christ, and
during her time there a number of students became
Christians. This thrilled her, and it increased her
longing for souls even more, and ever since.

The college consisted of 200 girls. The CU,
although fairly small, was strong and had a good mix

of denominations in its membership. This was one reason why Peggy had chosen to go to the college. The CU arranged trips to the Derby Youth For Christ rallies, and it was there that many of the girls were converted.

The college divinity lectures were not evangelical in tone, but God used them to make Peggy think, and to test her beliefs. The result was that she became a stronger Christian than before. We enjoyed our fellowship together as we talked over her lectures, and we went on long walks over the Derbyshire hills. More and more I felt that I wanted to spend my life with her, but she was not desperate for a boyfriend. In fact, as our relationship deepened, she found difficulty in coping with my increasing love. She later described our walks to her fellow students as rather like going out with her uncle! She would go back to college and get up to the most ridiculous antics to let off steam. I was serious, but she was frivolous – she even wore ankle socks!

I soon discovered that Peggy had long-standing problems with doubts about her salvation, so much of our time was spent on that subject. Since then we have ministered to many other Christians who have the same problem. Our experience stood us in good stead.

This was how God began to join us together.

3

God's Ruthless Love

God continued to shape us as we continued our
college courses, partly through our fellowship with
one another. Peggy is very different from me, and
her opinions about Scripture made me think over my
beliefs, and to some extent change those which I had
merely absorbed because the elders had preached
them. Similarly, my concept of God was much more
personal than Peggy's, so that changed her, too.

God is out to change us all the time, and he is very
set in his purpose—quite ruthless in fact! The word
'ruthless' is not commonly used in connection with
God, so let me give some meanings of it here. The
Old English word 'ruth' meant 'pity' or 'compassion'.
'Ruthless' means 'without pity in seeking a goal'. Other
meanings are 'firm', 'straight', 'strong', 'disciplined'.
When God has a goal in mind, he is strong in his
intention to achieve it. He does not deviate from it
and is courageous enough to put up with our accusation that he is without pity. So when I use the word
'ruthless' to describe God, I do not imply that he is
cruel—rather the reverse. He is loving, but not

sentimental. He is determined to make us like his
Son. Nothing in heaven, on earth, or in hell will ever
change his intention. It is irrevocable. He is set on
transforming us into kings and queens in heaven,
because his perspective is ever an eternal one. He has
ordained our blessing in this life; he begrudges us
nothing that will do us good; he is not a miser doling
out bare necessities of life. When he gives, he gives
like a king. But his plan for us goes far beyond this
life. He intends us to reign as King and queens in
heaven. In fact Scripture declares that 'if we have
only hoped in Christ in this life, we are of all men
most to be pitied' (1 Cor 15:19). The Bible also says
'God has set eternity in man's heart' (Ecc 3:11). How
then can man be satisfied with blessing on earth
alone?

Because many people realise that there is an eternal
aspect to their being, and that they need to know
something about it here and now, they are dabbling
in the occult. I believe it was Augustine who wrote,
'There is a God-shaped [eternal] void in man's heart,
which only God can fill.' Drinking, drugs, pop music,
immorality are the world's substitutes for the craving
after God and eternal values. They do not fit the
'void'; they do not satisfy. How can they?—for they
are temporal and man is eternal.

Through the years we have been to night clubs,
youth clubs, pubs, and dance halls to try to reach
young people with the message of eternity, the gospel
which alone can satisfy the God-implanted desire for
fulfilment. There were hardened sinners among
them: girls and boys of twelve and thirteen who were
expert prostitutes; teenagers with old faces ravaged
from drug abuse, and crooks galore. They were all
looking for excitement, satisfaction, or an identity of

some sort, even though it was that of a thug. None of
them would admit to a belief in God, but they all
hoped that there was something somewhere which
would satisfy them more than anything they had
experienced so far in this life. I used to pray, 'O God,
help them into their proper destiny, and deliver them
from the deceit of the Enemy.' Some of them began
to understand a little of the truth, but the jeers of
their fellows, and the cost of the Cross, made most of
them draw back.

Christian life is far from easy, but, because God is
set on our eternal greatness in heaven, he will lovingly
allow us to endure all kinds of tribulation on earth if it
results in our greater joy and glory in heaven. If
sculptors use a sharp chisel and a heavy mallet to
conform the stone to the image in their minds, should
not God be allowed to use sharp and heavy things in
order to realise in us what he ever wanted before the
world began? He has the right, and he makes use of
it: to shape people and situations in order to knock
off our sharp corners, and to mould us into the
likeness of his dear Son. If man is so determined to
have his own way, should not God have an equal
right? And if man does not deviate from his way, why
should God deviate from his intention?

Having digressed a little to stress an important
point, let me now get back to our story.

The end of one era; start of the next

In 1955 the Bible college moved to Teignmouth, and
my course came to an end. I had hoped to go abroad
as a missionary, and I badly wanted to go to Ethiopia,
but I could not for health reasons. I was bitterly
disappointed, and I had a real crisis of conviction as

to whether God truly loved me. I felt he had let me
down and had not noticed all the sacrifices I had
made for his sake. So, not really knowing what to do,
I returned at the end of 1955 to Matlock, where
Peggy was in her final year at the training college. I
settled down again with the Brethren Assembly, who
gave me a warm welcome. One of the dear godly
women there, whom we called Aunty Wright, gave
me lodgings in her home, and we had great times of
fellowship together. She shared my burden for other
lands.

Seeing that my work in the assembly was voluntary,
and that I was a growing lad, financial needs clam-
oured, so I looked for a job. I could not find one for
quite a while, and during this time God renewed my
training in faith. This is another of God's favourite
lessons for his heirs, and it can only be learned
through difficult or impossible circumstances.
Hebrews 11 is full of examples of his intention to
teach it, cost what it might, to his people. (He allowed
some to be killed, testing their faith in his care and
love to the utmost. Others had to roam the earth clad
only in skins.)

Faith is so precious to God, and so vital to his
people, that he will determinedly subject them to all
kinds of trial. Didn't he do the same with his own
great Son? Faith is God's chosen route to a powerful
church. He shaped his people and taught them faith
then—and he does it now. He taught some by allowing persecution: others, like me, by a boring laboratory job. Scriptures—true, but not fulfilled in every
individual's life—can almost torment us, and God
does not always step in quickly to alleviate our pain.
Instead he lets us grow in faith through them. Irritating people alongside us can also be God's means of

teaching us faith and perseverance. Many are the 'tools' in his box, and whether he uses the chisel or the mallet, his eternal intention is the same, that we should be 'conformed to the image of his dear Son' (Rom 8:29).

The only job I could find at this time involved selling potato crisps to the pubs in Derbyshire. This brought a conflict in my heart because I had been brought up to believe that such places were dens of iniquity. I prayed that God would not let me sink to such depths, especially after going to a Bible college! But God had more courage than I did, and he said I should take the job. So I did. It was all part of his gracious, ruthless dealings, for I soon lost my remaining bigotry, and was able to reach out to many of the people I met there who wanted to know about God.

Several of the landlords and ladies found Jesus through me. One of them was an ex-Regimental Sergeant Major in the Coldstream Guards, about seven feet tall and weighing eighteen stones. His pub was crowded with hard-looking men, all swearing. Something I said showed him that I was 'one of those **** Bible thumpers'. I was trying to sell him a jar of pickles because I received good commission on those, but he ignored my sales pitch and, picking me up with one hand, hauled me over the bar. He roared out 'Hey lads, we've got a *** vicar here.' They all cheered and swore, then mine host said, 'Well, give us a *** sermon then.' I was terrified, but God in his grace took over and enabled me to preach in a way that brought conviction and tears to many. When I had finished, I had to leave because my lunch hour was over. Looking for the landlord, I found him sobbing in the back room; he told me in highly coloured language to clear off saying, 'My mother was like you. You are right, but get the *** out.' Realising that I would not be selling him any pickles, I went.

Another encounter was with a lady owner. She was the archetypal buxom, blonde, brassy barmaid. She must have been a bit desperate because she started to 'chat me up'. When she saw that I was not playing, she cursed me out of the pub. So I went. A week later I called again, and when she saw me, she screamed out, 'Go away, go away, you must be God.' She had the common notion that God is a vengeful God, and that he had come to punish her for cursing me. I assured her that I was not God, but Alex Buchanan, and she calmed down and told me that after I had left previously, her little girl had gone out to play and had fallen into the canal and drowned. I was able to talk to her about Jesus, and she was born again.

At this time I was courting Peggy, and I needed money to buy an engagement ring. My salesmanship was about as successful as a mouse selling catfood, so I prayed hard and visited a pub. This hotel, called the Black Bull Inn, had a landlord who would have made Scrooge seem like a philanthropist; he usually bought one tin of crisps, and then wanted commission. But this time, due to God's grace and very little else, he bought all my stock of crisps! I drove home quickly and took Peggy to Derby. Metaphorically speaking, I swopped the crisps for diamonds! Our celebration meal was of egg and chips in Smith's Cafe. We were so happy—and broke!

I had fallen in love with Peggy before she really loved me. She can tell her side of the story here.

'When I first met Alex, he was very serious, and he thought I was rather frivolous and light-hearted, but I say that I was an optimist with a sense of fun. I liked to impersonate people as I did with a school friend who was unwell. I put my school scarf over the phone and pretended to be his girlfriend; his father insisted on meeting this mimic, so I was invited to his party. My success went too far! This kind of thing happened often I'm afraid. I had a good strong father, and I think Alex was a kind of father figure to me initially. I was attracted by his strength of mind and purpose. But his tenderness was even more important to me. One evening we were walking along the banks of the Mersey in Cheadle, and as we talked, I saw that gentle tenderness in his eyes. I knew then that I loved him and wanted to marry him. Thirty-five years later we are still deeply in love, and my sense of fun has matured. Alex is not so serious either! We praise God for one another.'

Eventually I needed a better job, so I looked around for a long time before the managing director of a nearby firm offered me a job in the laboratory. I told him honestly that I had never done any chemistry at school, nor was I good at maths, and that I could not remember the boiling point of water. He roared with laughter and told me to start on Monday! How gracious God is; especially to the 'weak and foolish'.

I learned some more gloriously irritating lessons there, such as how to deal with difficult people and circumstances. If we are puzzled by the fact that an irritating person lives or works alongside us, the answer could be as simple as this—God put him or her there, in his ruthless love! Such a man worked in the same laboratory as I did. I'll call him Francis (not his real name).

He disliked me from the start, and when he realised I was a Christian, his dislike grew into hatred.

One day he was so angry with me that he threw a heavy tin of tarmacadam at me. It missed me by a hair's-breadth, and I thus deduced that he was not very friendly; unfortunately, I lost my temper and threw it back at him. I missed him, too. Later God spoke to me through that annoying verse: 'Blessed are you when men revile you and persecute you . . .' (Mt 5:11). I remember murmuring to God that I did not feel very blessed; then God told me to pray for him! I knew that God was not joking, so I tried.

Through gritted teeth I prayed, 'Lord, please bless Francis, if it is possible to bless Francis. I don't really want him to be blessed but this is the way to pray, I suppose.'

My quiet times were very quiet for a while; but God does not give up, so I prayed again. Once again God ungritted my teeth, and my heart began to warm to Francis. The next day God gave me grace to make Francis a cup of tea, which he promptly poured down the sink. I made him another with the same result. Calculating that seventy times seven would use up quite a number of teabags, I left it for the moment, went away and had a quiet weep. But as God helped me and I accepted his help, the relationship changed into friendship. As far as I know he is not saved to this day, but God taught me that he was quite determined to make me more like his Son—lovingly persistent.

Married!

Because the Assembly was engaged in building a new chapel at that time, we could not be married there. Thus, in December 1957, we were married in Cheadle Parish Church where Peggy had lived. The vows became very real to me later on when Peggy

became ill. 'In sickness and in health' is so wonderfully binding, and rehearsing it at intervals is
helpful. We set up home in Matlock, where our three
lovely children were born.

Our home became a haven for local students.
Knowing how much we had appreciated Christian
hospitality ourselves, we were glad to make this a part
of our lives. Peggy would bake cakes far into the night
as part of this caring, then she would do her ironing,
plus preparation for teaching! She was a bundle of
energy in those days, sacrificial in the way she cared
for me and the students. Peggy would talk to some of
them and counsel them while she fed the children,
and I would make the others wash the dishes as we
talked in the kitchen about the Lord. So 'a talk with
Alex in the kitchen' became not only a family joke,
but a part of our ministry to them.

As we were the only young couple in the fellowship,
our friends were mostly older than we were, and we
learned such a lot from these older saints. One of
them, Aunty Wright, was like a third grandma to our
children. She loved the Lord so much, and she had a
real missionary vision, which helped to keep our
vision alive. Many of the visiting missionaries stayed
in our home, and, because of Peggy's zeal, she
attended a missionary meeting concerning the Mau
Mau in Kenya. At the closing appeal, people were
asked to stand up if they were willing to go to Kenya
should God ask them to do so.

Peggy stood up, prepared to go as far as she knew
her heart. Later people said how brave they thought
she was, seeing that, by then, she was a young mother
with three children. But she had reasoned that if God
called, she would just have to go. (God knew her
heart, and, after about a year, he was indeed to call

her—plus the family—though not to Kenya, but to
Liverpool! It would be a terrible wrench from beautiful Matlock to a terraced house in Liverpool's city
centre. Peggy was to find the move far from easy, but
as she says 'I had stood up to say I would follow God
wherever he led me, hadn't I?')

After some years my laboratory job became boring
and repetitive, and I confess that I wanted to get out,
but God in his grace kept me there, and taught me so
much about patience and persistence. The job also
paid the bills. I had another operation and more
health problems, but Peggy was still full of health and
energy.

The quest for healing

Healing is a many-sided concept, and when I use the
term in a general sense, I mean wholeness: of mind,
emotion, and spirit—even wholeness in attitudes. By
God's grace Peggy and I had largely found wholeness
in our emotions and attitudes, but not in our bodies.
In this part of the book, therefore, 'healing' means
physical healing.

My health became worse, and I wondered whether
there was anyone nearby who healed the sick. A
friend told me of a healing meeting in London and
offered to take me there, together with my college
friend Tim Donovan. I agreed, and we duly arrived
at the meeting hall. The healer turned out to be an
excitable gentleman, who was assisted by his four
beautiful daughters. After his sermon we formed a
healing line and waited our turn.

His technique was to line up his four daughters on
the platform, and get them to elicit our particular
needs, which they then passed on to him. Arriving in

front of these beautiful creatures, I told them one by one that I was deaf, facially paralysed, and in awful pain. They told their father who took my head in his hands while screwing my ears round and round. He then muttered in a tongue, drew a deep breath, bellowed out, 'In the name of Jesus'—and hurled me off the platform. While I was sitting in a heap, meditating on the significance of this new method of healing, my friend arrived in a heap beside me on the floor. He was more bruised than I was, and far from pleased with the healer. So ended another excursion into the realm of the healers.

We decided that we might as well get on with the work of the Assembly, health or no health, so we helped them to build a new church, ran the Covenanters, gave hospitality to nearly all the visiting speakers and missionaries etc. In addition our house was still full every Sunday with students from the college.

The quest for power

Despite my health problems our life was full and we were happy together, but there was still a nagging ache in my heart. The Scriptures in Acts tormented me, because I knew there was a spiritual power that I still did not have in my life. I loved God, but he was not real enough to me as a Person.

I fasted, prayed, cried, yearned, disciplined my flesh, did every legalistic thing I could in order to persuade the Spirit to give me this power and fruitfulness that I saw in the Bible. But all to no avail. I grew more depressed, and wondered if I would ever be different.

About this time I heard of the Ruanda Mission, and

one of their teams came to Swanwick Conference Centre nearby. Peggy persuaded me to go along to the open day. There I discovered the truth of the old hymn 'It is not try, but trust'. Roy Hession, Fred Barf, and Bishop Barham prayed me out of my legalism, and life was immediately sweeter. I also felt Jesus much nearer and more real to me as a Person. How gracious God is to lead us at a pace we can stand.

Our Sundays were far from being a day of rest; I was up early to pray, then we had a small prayer meeting, then on to the morning meeting, the Covenanters; home for a bite, then the old people's home meeting, followed by the open air meeting; evening meeting and home again to entertain the students. I began to wonder if Jesus worked as hard as this, and I discovered that he worked just as hard, but far more economically. Reading John 5:19 and 30 convinced me that I was more of a zealous employee for God than a co-worker. In his grace, God began to speak to me about the danger of 'uncommanded work', and I felt a great longing to walk even more closely to him so that I could just do what *he* told me to do, instead of responding to every need which confronted me; I realised that Satan can engineer some of these supposed needs. However, I was still unsatisfied and frustrated because I did not see the power of God in my life and ministry, and I could not find in my Christian service the same economy of working with God that I saw in the ministry of Jesus.

Again, in his grace, God brought Denis Clark, from Worthing, to our Assembly. He spoke about something called the baptism in the Spirit, of which I had not heard. At first, like the other elders, I felt very suspicious, and wanted to 'pray' him out of the town. Peggy also was very nervous of the whole thing, but largely because she did not feel ready for such an experience. But as we listened, I began to see that this experience was what I wanted and needed. Later on, we had a meeting for those who wanted this blessing, and I thought 'I don't care what they call it—I want this.'

Many of the people who were prayed for began to weep, laugh, rejoice, speak in strange language—all except me. We adjourned to our larger house (God had given it to us by a semi-miracle by then), and more were blessed—except for me. I was livid, and 'rejoiced' with the others by means of sheer hypocrisy. After they had all gone I went up to the attic and began to howl and scream with frustration.

Again I want to point out that our lovingly ruthless Father will allow us to be frustrated until we are desperate enough, in a right sense of the word, for the blessing of his power. God has the right to deal with us like this. In my case he had allowed me to live on borrowed time. The One who lends has the right to stipulate the terms. He has all the caring determination of the surgeon, who knows that he must push in the knife despite the possible fear or resistance of the patient, if he is to bring life and health.

Eventually, feeling utterly hopeless, I cried out, 'O God, this baptism in the Holy Spirit is sheer unadulterated rubbish; it's bunkum.' At that precise moment I was suffused with the power of God; I saw a vision of Jesus which has never left me; I spoke in tongues, but that was secondary to the major experience. I fell deeply in love with the Son of God, and became a new man. The glow remained for a long time, and I had never been so happy. Those at work noticed it, and it was difficult for me to concentrate on the job. I kept giggling all the time and often had to rush out of the laboratory for a quick outburst of mirth. No wonder they looked at me askance. They already thought I was mad!

All those who had been filled with the Spirit gathered in our home to seek God further; Denis helped us a lot by letter, and we staggered on trying to learn as we went, but because there was so little teaching about at that time, we gradually subsided into the ordinary. There followed some of the darkest days of my Christian life. I became ill again; the family was suffering in various ways; the elders did not understand or appreciate what had happened to me. We could not find anyone to help us. But God in his grace held us up and kept us going.

Oh, not again!

One consolation in those difficult days was that we lived in the country, which we loved. One day, during this time, Peggy and I were walking along a lovely country lane enjoying the peace and serenity of country life. It was so different from the frenetic pace of the city of London where I was born, and I very much wanted to stay in the country. I said to her 'Darling, I never want to live in a city again.' I should have kept my mouth shut! Six months later, God called me into 'full-time work' right near the centre of Liverpool. I tried praying my prayer in reverse, but it didn't work!

This move came about through an experience one day in 1963; I was walking home along the bank of the river Derwent, and I suddenly felt that I could not go on. I reminded the Lord that he had called me to 'full-time work' years before, and said 'Lord, you *must* show me what to do; either take this desire away, or

fulfil it please.' When I got home, Peggy said, 'Ken
(Terhoven) asked me to tell you to write to the
superintendent of the Liverpool City Mission.' I did,
and within a few months we were there.

Peggy writes, 'When Ken had asked me to tell Alex
that the Superintendent of the Liverpool City Mission
was interested in him, I knew in my heart that we
would be accepted and move to that city. The following day is one I still recall clearly. Our daughter Ruth
was at school; the boys were having their morning
sleep; and I was washing the kitchen floor. I began to
think, counting the cost of such a move. Liverpool
was then receiving bad publicity, and the TV pictures
were anything but reassuring. But because I loved
God, I went there, though as an obedient servant
more than as a joyful daughter of God.'

4

God's Fierce Flame

Hark to Love's triumphant shout!
'Joy is born from pain,
Joy is sorrow inside out,
Grief remade again.
Broken hearts look up and see
This is Love's own victory.'

Here marred things are made anew,
Filth is here made clean,
Here are robes, not rags, for you,
Mirth where tears have been.
Where sin's dreadful power was found,
Grace doth now much more abound.

Hark! such songs of jubilation!
Every creature sings,
Great the joy of every nation,
'LOVE is King of kings,
See, ye blind ones! shout, ye dumb!
Joy is sorrow overcome.'

Hannah Hurnard

When we left Matlock in 1964 and moved to
Liverpool, we were commended by the elders into

what they called 'full-time work'. It is a silly term, because every Christian is full time. Perhaps those who are set apart to the pastoral ministry are really 'overtime workers'! Certainly we were entering one of the busiest eras of our life together.

We had left a lovely house overlooking an orchard, with views right down the Derwent Valley. I had a good job, and was about to be promoted. Here we had a terraced house with no garden in a fairly grubby area of the city. No wonder Peggy and I had spent the night before we moved telling each other all the silly jokes we could think of! The move was a sacrifice, but small in comparison to those made by many others.

I would not have chosen to live in Liverpool, but when God moves us from a place, it is no longer home; instead the new place becomes home. God teaches some things in one situation, then commands us to move to another, so that he can do different things to and through us there; static Christians are not always well-rounded spiritually.

Liverpool was also, for us, a place of further testing. I like the oft-told story of the goldsmith who, when asked how he knew that the gold in his crucible was pure enough, answered, 'When I can see my face in it.' That is precisely God's intention in his dealings with us. This simple answer explains God's dealings with us very well. When one era of life, or time in the crucible, is over, God moves us into the next. He is always doing something, and always going some-where. There is nothing static about God; therefore his dealings with us are continuous—unless we opt out, or dig our heels in. If we do opt out, then because he is a courteous God, he will press on with other people until we come to our senses. And when we repent, he will resume what he was doing with us in the first place. To go back to the crucible illustration, I have found that when I feel reasonably satisfied with the purity of my 'gold', God does not always feel the same.

God's satisfaction is far more important than ours. He is never satisfied with that which is partial, and there are no half measures with him. So he turns the heat up to reveal some more impurities in us. This can be devastating if we misunderstand what he is doing. We can easily lose heart and start to reason in our mind that we will never be pure enough, so there is no point in going on. In fact, if we are not careful, this testing can cause us to become obsessed with our sin; a perpetual spiritual 'hand-washing'. There is no need to be so morbid; we need to rejoice in the progress God has made in our lives, and to joyfully submit to more heat because of the supreme pleasure of greater Christlikeness.

Not only does God's testing produce the purer gold of holy character, it also makes us more useful and usable to him. The Joseph of Genesis 37 and 38 is a good illustration. At first a spoiled child with a high opinion of himself, he, through the testing of slavery, false accusation, imprisonment and loneliness, plus the delay and the 'testing of the word of God' (Ps 105:19), became qualified to be the saviour of the nation—its virtual leader. God tried him, trusted him, tested him again, allowed more delay, then brought him out of prison in order to save not only the land of Egypt, but also the nation of Israel.

Because God had purer gold in mind for us (though not the same job), he moved us on to this city, where he could turn up the heat. For some while we were without a home there; Peggy and the children

lived with her parents in Cheadle, while I lodged in
the Mission deaconess' house. We could not find a
house to buy for a long time, and this, together with
the separation and the lack of money, put us to a
number of tests immediately. We wondered if we had
made a mistake, especially when we read glowing
testimonies of the 'prosperity' preachers. Their guidance seemed so miraculous, and everything seemed
to be laid on for them. Apparently they moved
straight into their homes, and everything was easy.
Then we re-read the Bible passages where Paul spoke
of his trials, and the account of Jesus who had
nowhere to lay his head, and we were reassured.

Every step of our guidance was tested at this time.
Finances were low; the children's school was far from
ideal—bullies abounded in it; the work was different
from that in Matlock, with much heavier responsibilities thrust upon us at bewildering speed. The neighbours were a test too, for they did not like these
'foreign snobs'. The area was vastly different from
beautiful Matlock, and not far from one of the worst
areas of the city. When we and the neighbours really
got to know each other, we found that the Liverpool
people were great, and they in turn began to like us,
but it was certainly a difficult time. The heat was *up*, at
about 220°C!

Eventually we bought the house in which I first
lodged, and the family were united again. I spent
much of the first year in my overalls, for there was so
much to do both in the house and in the dilapidated
church. One evening after I had knocked down an
interior wall and was covered in dust, a couple
knocked at the door. Seeing the dirty, dishevelled
figure answering their knock, they hesitantly asked if
I was the vicar of Jubilee Chapel. I reassured them

that I was, so they asked if I would marry them. I said, 'If you are both Christians, yes. But if one is not, then I won't. So are you both Christians?' They said 'Yes.' I knew they were not, so I said to the man, 'If you drop dead now, you will go straight to hell.' He nearly fainted and cried out in fear, 'I don't want to go there.' From then on it was a plain, simple job to lead him to Christ, and shortly afterwards the girl was born again too. That was a happy marriage!

First pastorate

The church of which I was to be pastor was a worldly and disordered place where some of the leaders were not even Christians. Its traditions were anything but spiritual, and when I began to insist on biblical principles and godliness of life, the heat was certainly turned up yet again.

I always find confrontation distressing, but God uses these situations to refine us and teach us many lessons, such as patience, grace, boldness, faith etc.

Some of the choir members, though not all, were unspiritual. They caused so much anguish that the only thing to do, after much prayer and fasting on our part, was to remove the choir pews. Their faces when they went to sit down were a picture, and the whole church held its breath, but because we had prayed so much, and God heard and responded, they repented and quietly sat elsewhere. This opened a new era in which we began to see blessing in the church.

My work was to be the pastor of the headquarters church of the Mission, and, in addition, to minister to down-and-out men. These men were used by God to test everything we had ever learned about wisdom and discernment. They told wonderful stories about their exploits and how the state had treated them so shabbily. Some of them spent a lot of time in and around our home until we learned the difference between sense and sacrifice, and became more selective. More than once I literally carried these men on my back to the nearest hostel, because they were stone drunk.

On some occasions we scrubbed them down and reclothed them because their own clothes walked away on their own! We fed them, told them about Jesus, loved them, got them out of jail, found them jobs, and so on. Not many of them were saved, because they did not *want* to be saved. Most of them got where they were by addiction to alcohol. In many cases this addiction had begun through social drinking, required in the nature of their business. Eventually they had been mastered by it, and their lives fell in ruins. Some though were different. One man had been a respected doctor, who, when asked to perform abortions for the local prostitutes, refused. The women came back, this time with their pimps, armed with knives. They threatened to murder his wife and children, so eventually he gave up and left home in despair. When some missioners eventually discovered him, he was crouching in a shop doorway trying to cook a lump of fat bacon on a shovel over a candle. We took him in, loved and helped him, witnessed to him, but three weeks later he died. God taught us a lot about his compassion through these experiences. No wonder we were put through the mill as never before in those Liverpool days.

We pastored the church, ministered to down-and-out men, preached in the docks and on the ships, manned the suicide line on the phone, sometimes

ministered in the prisons, and visited in hospitals.
Most of the Mission staff had a similar workload, so
we were not unique. The dockers were interested in
us, but not our preaching. Sometimes they would
throw things at us and abuse us, but some listened,
and later found the Lord. At the open-air meetings
on the pier head, which I dreaded, the local Secular
Society would cluster around us like a flock of vul-
tures, but again God overruled and brought some to
salvation, mostly through other men, not through
me.

As God turned up the heat in Liverpool, we were
changed even more, and we learned fresh things, too.
We learned to spot spongers a mile away, and to turn
away from some of them in case we engaged in
uncommanded work. After all, Jesus did!

Fear of man; fear of God

At this time I was forbidden to preach about what the
Liverpool City Mission Committee called 'pentecostal
things'. And, like a fool, I obeyed. My preaching
around this period could be described as 'driving
Pharaoh's chariot with the wheels off'. There was
some blessing, but not much. A very few conversions,
but little else.

The conflict in my heart about the Holy Spirit grew
and grew. I wanted to obey the Committee by refrain-
ing from preaching about the baptism in the Spirit,
but I knew that I was grieving the Spirit by so doing. I
was so torn that I felt on the brink of a breakdown.
Added to this was the verdict of a specialist that in his
view I might not be around in a year or so because of
a dangerous infection near my brain. Also about this
time Peggy was beginning to feel very weak and tired.
She was experiencing numbness in her body and had

trouble with her hands. It was hardly surprising that she was tired, for, apart from being ill, she was a pastor's wife, leader of the women's meeting, mother of three small children, and a teacher at school. She has never been lazy! All these things weighed so heavily on us that we had to take a month's leave of absence in order to think out our future, and whether we could carry on at all.

Mercifully the Lord led me to some Christian men in the South who gave me the word of the Lord. This word was so painful that I broke down in an agony of conviction. I wept and wept, wondering if God would ever forgive me for refusing to preach the *whole* counsel of God. Then I saw a clear vision of Jesus again, this time as though my spittle was running down his face because by my cowardice, I had really spat in his face. It was a most awful thing to see the holiness of God in the face of his Son; nothing breaks a man as this does. First you think you will die, then you fear that you won't. But then, praise God, he smiled at me. He said 'I have forgiven you, Alex.' I cannot describe the following moments; they are too hallowed. Suffice it to say that God is a God of inexhaustible grace.

We came back to the chapel, and God brought wave after wave of blessing to us. Preaching consisted simply of opening the Bible, and the Spirit took over. I preached the baptism of the Spirit month after month, and many of the people entered into new blessing. This was opposed by some, both inside and outside the chapel, and sadly, many of those who opposed it became bitter and eventually stopped attending the church.

Blessing always brings crises, and we had more than our share of them. After a small operation on my head which left me unable to take the weekly prayer and Bible study meeting, a visiting preacher somehow got into that meeting, and he came to the front and began to preach the old heresy about sinless perfection. He brought so-called words of knowledge which supposedly exposed serious sin in about 90% of the congregation. He said that there were only two real Christians in the church, and he was one them! Furthermore, he preached that you could not be saved unless you were baptised in the Spirit. As a result of this heretical stuff the fellowship was confused, damaged, and divided. Divisions arose between the leaders, and the flow of blessing slowed. Further complications arose from the Committee, and life became grim again. I looked earnestly for a mature man who understood these things to counsel me and stand by us, but although many were ready with platitudes and advice, no one brought us counsel from God. In fact, few men even listened. ('Pastors have very few pastors!')

God called me back to earnest prayer, which I had neglected because blessing had previously been so abundant in the church. After many weeks of this, blessing began to return to the meetings, and God began to restructure them. Instead of me being the kingpin, an eldership was formed, and open worship instituted. Spiritual gifts were manifested, and we prospered. It was a bit nerve wracking, because whereas I had previously worked everything out in detail, and knew where we were going, now it was anybody's guess what would happen in the meetings. But the people grew in gifting, and in godliness. Peggy and I love them still, and we owe them so much for their love and patience. They have now formed into two independent fellowships in the city. Old

Swan Christian Fellowship; Wavertree Christian Fellowship; now called Earlsfield.

My early prophesying

It was during this time in Jubilee Chapel that God first caused me to prophesy. This was followed with other prophecies elsewhere in the city, some of which had remarkable results. Clear, detailed revelation was given in one church about some future events in the city, and this was fulfilled in detail on the date specified in the prophecy. Similar things have been revealed to me ever since.

My quiet times were probably of a high standard, but God required an even higher one now—far more of my time. He caused me to get up at dawn day after day in order to wait on him. Physically speaking, this nearly killed me; it curtailed my other activities drastically. In turn this led to some misunderstanding with the Committee who had employed me to be busy all day in obvious work. Some of my colleagues also looked askance at this apparent superspirituality, but there was no other way. When a King speaks, his subjects obey.

Peggy was still teaching in the local school, although she found it increasingly difficult to do so. Our children found things hard, too, for some of the local people felt that we were a cut above them. Their children taunted ours saying, 'Yar, just 'cos yer mum's a teacher, and yer dad owns that chapel. . .' One boy was heard to tell his mother that I was very rich: 'Mum, every Sunday he gets two huge bags of money given to him in the service.' If only he knew! Wages in the Mission were low, and there was no overtime pay!

Our children were young at this time. The boys were not too aware that there was anything wrong with their mother, but Ruth began to get worried from time to time, for she was a thoughtful girl and understood some of her mum's problems. Some fears entered her heart as to how we would cope if mum got worse, and if MS was hereditary. Her faith began to be tested.

All change

Having spent some years training the elders, and seeing them take more and more of the load, I began to feel that God was loosening the strings that held me to the Mission. I went for refreshment to a conference which was called a prayer and Bible week, but found myself involved in personal ministry to many people there. I had not expected this at all, but my heart responded to such a conference, so I took my family to the next one.

That conference turned out to be one of the most significant events of my life. I went again simply to listen and learn, but I found myself preaching there more than anyone else! This was due to the grace of Denis Clark, who founded these prayer and Bible weeks. At the end of the week, Peggy, realising that something dramatic was happening, and that God was redirecting us, asked Denis to pray for her so that she would in no way hinder what God was doing in me. So Denis and others prayed over me, gave me a clear prophetic word, and commended me to the wider ministry which God had showed them. I was dumbfounded, but Peggy was not surprised, she knew it was God's plan. So we went home rejoicing but a bit tremulous. There followed many invitations to preach all over the place—so many in fact, that it

proved increasingly difficult to fulfil them and still be
the pastor at Jubilee Chapel.

Peggy bore the brunt of many of our tough experiences in the years which followed, very few of which
are mentioned in this book. She put up with my times
of deep despair, and my irritation. She kept our
home together; she kept me sane; she kept our
children blessed and guarded. What a wife! Going to
Liverpool had been a shock for us both, but particularly for her after living in Matlock.

Peggy endued with power

Peggy was baptised in the Spirit while we lived in
Liverpool. She tells the story in her own words:

'Much was said about the baptism in the Spirit at
this time. It was controversial and dangerous. But
whereas I was afraid of the subject when we were in
Matlock, I was now hungry for this empowering
experience. I began to seek God earnestly, and to ask
questions. Eventually Alex asked a lady called Joan
Porter to come and talk to me about it. We talked for
a long time, and she shared her own experience some
years before. Eventually she prayed for me as I knelt
by our studio couch. As she prayed, my heart was
flooded with a sense of God's presence. I had never
known anything so beautiful; I didn't want to get up
from my knees; I did not want to lose it because it was
so precious.

'Joan slipped out of the room, but I stayed for a
long time in the presence of the Lord I loved. For
three weeks afterwards I basked in the love of God. It
was like a spiritual honeymoon; words are too inade-
quate to describe it. At times Alex and I were pros-
trate on the floor in wonderful worship and

adoration. If we went out in the car, we would be talking about God, and laughing with sheer joy as we did so. It was wonderful. But it was as yet untested!

'Some weeks later Satan violently attacked my mind. Foul and wicked thoughts assailed me and left me feeling desolate, confused, and guilty. Where had they come from? Surely I was not secretly depraved! I could not remember gross sin in my life, so why this all of a sudden? Looking back now I wish I had been more conversant with the account of the temptation of Jesus in the wilderness. His Father had just declared from heaven, "This is my beloved Son in whom I am well pleased." Then, Satan immediately assailed him with every weapon he had to persuade him to deny the testimony of the Father. Well, I should have known! If Jesus experienced such things, surely we will, too.

'When I discussed my experience with Alex, he told me that after his renewing in the Spirit, he experienced similar things, usually during a Communion service. At first he wanted to run because he felt utterly disqualified from serving God with such foul things in his mind. But God gave him wisdom to see that these things did not come from within; they were hurled into his mind from outside. So we both learned at such times to lift the thoughts to God and say, "Lord, these things have nothing to do with me; I neither mean them, nor do I want them; I destroy them now in Jesus' Name." We commend it. It works.'

Peggy becomes ill

Peggy had married me knowing that I was deaf, but this was no problem for her at first, because she was then strong, healthy, and could hear normally. She

saw no problem in coping. She would be my ears and
help me. It was a terrible shock when she became ill
herself. She prayed frequently and in anguish, 'O
Lord, where are you?' Then, because she is a buoyant
person, she would say, 'Never mind, I will cope.' This
was her experience through the ensuing years. With
hindsight, we can see what God was doing in her. She
thought she was doing so well as a Christian, and she
was. But the last twenty-seven years have been a
school where she has come to know the Lord more
truly—although she realises that she has not gradu-
ated yet!

During 1966 to 1971, Peggy saw a gradual deterioration in her health. The doctors could not diagnose
the problem; at that time doctors were reluctant to
give a comparatively young person a diagnosis
anyway. They preferred to wait for a second episode
before giving it a name.

Because of this, she felt that she must find out for
herself what was wrong, and when it was finally
diagnosed as MS it was almost a relief. Looking back
on it now, we realise that her dedicated search for a
name or diagnosis was not faith building. Years later,
a Christian doctor recognised this and said, 'Peggy, I
am sorry that we (the medical profession) ever gave
you a diagnosis, for it is like giving you a life
sentence.' She could only reply 'Don't apologise,
because we patients do demand a name for our ills.'

It is difficult to prevent the name of the illness from
sinking into the heart, and from hindering faith.
However, God is gracious, and determined to form
the image of his Son in us. Step by step he has led us
both until we can believe that all things really do work
together for good to those who love him, and are
called according to his purpose.

How did we cope with bringing up the family? As we write, we are keenly aware that there are many people who have suffered far more than Peggy has, and that there are children who have had to bear a far heavier burden than ours have done. We can only thank God for his grace to Peggy. We tried to keep things on a light level for the children's sake; Peggy wore long-sleeved dresses to hide the bruises from continual blood tests. We think it was useful to give young doctors experience in puncturing real people rather than oranges!

At one stage she needed a stick to walk and then she did the shopping by pushing a child's pushchair with a bag tied to it for balance. In the home, strategically placed furniture provided support for Peggy. It was difficult for her to cross the lounge, but the boys, who would lie on the floor to watch TV, would obligingly put up a foot or an arm for Peggy to hang on to. This all helped keep life fairly normal. It is said that children from a home in which someone is disabled are more understanding than usual. This is certainly the case with ours.

Each loss of ability brought its own pangs, but Peggy's cheerfulness and determination that the family would not suffer made her grateful to God for all that she could do. People gave us prophetic words and pictures. Several of them 'saw' Peggy walking and running. But just as it is possible to learn to live with sickness, it is (sadly) possible to live with 'prophecies'. Such prophecies can feed unbelief, and induce guilt, causing us to think that the fault is ours when we do not see their fulfilment.

When suddenly Peggy could no longer walk or stand, one of our sons said, 'Mother, I think God has allowed this to make you take healing seriously. Your trouble is that you are a coper.' This made us smile; of course we took healing seriously . . . or did we? We would ask God for help in various tasks, and indeed, for healing, but if physical healing did not come, we would conclude that it was not the time, and just get on with life. As Peggy said, 'I really had little time to get absorbed in whether or not I was healed.' However, we have gone back to the Lord many times asking him to reveal any sin, or anything else which could be holding up our healing. We firmly believe in healing, for the Bible says 'He forgives our sins and heals our diseases' (Ps 103:3). Peggy's basic health is good, but there is a need for a miracle so that she can walk. It is that miracle for which we are looking and waiting. God was again moving us from one crucible to another. Eventually, even more invitations to preach arrived from all over the place, though I did not seek them, and because it proved impossible to fulfil them and still be the pastor and a city missionary, I left the Mission and started the new work on April Fool's Day in 1973.

5

God's Baffling Silence

Sometimes God speaks very clearly to his people; at other times he says nothing at all. Occasionally he says 'no' or 'wait'. On other occasions he gives a word of encouragement but without specific guidance. At still other times, if we are spiritually mature, he leaves it to us to decide what to do or where to go. When God speaks clearly, it is easy to follow him; when he does not speak, it's hard. But when he does seem silent, or when he delays in answering us, it is always to teach us faith—never to tease or frustrate us.

A year or so after starting this new work, which obviously involved much travelling it became clear that we needed to move from Liverpool, so we sought God for guidance. I felt that we could move anywhere we wanted because we were mature enough for God to say, 'You may move wherever you like, and I will bless you.' In our earlier days of Christian life, God needed to give us 'fleeces', or very explicit guidance, as he did with Gideon, who was a baby in the ways of the Lord at that time in his career.

Peggy wanted a more direct guidance, and she

71

asked God for a sign from Scripture. God gave her
one, surely with a twinkle in his eye, from Jeremiah
40: 'The whole land is before you, go wherever it
seems convenient to you.' Peggy was quite cross, and
said, 'It's rather like being given the freedom of the
Sahara Desert!' However, we had a letter from
Harvey and Valerie Dean, our friends in York, who
said that there was a Buchanan-style house (large and
rambling) for sale there. At the same time we received
a cheque for £300, a larger amount than we had ever
received until then. We felt God was using these
circumstances to say 'Go to York.' So we went.

Greater faith demands that we pass through times
when God is silent. He was silent on many occasions
during our time in York. The wilderness is twin to the
oasis. The still waters in our 'oasis' times can lull us to
sleep; our 'valley of the shadow' times will keep us
alert. The man who refuses the difficult times is a
spiritual babe, and is not fit to rule in the final heaven.
Babies do not make very good kings! How can such a
man ever say that he has walked in the path which his
Master trod? Peggy and I are two of the thousands of
Christians who have trodden difficult paths, and we
esteem the privilege of doing so. The old hymn puts it
well: 'It was the path the Master trod. Should not his
servants tread it still?'

We do not like it when we feel baffled by a silent
Father, but God has neither changed nor abdicated.
Those who cannot believe this and trust him in the
dark have never really trusted him in the light. No
wonder God is silent sometimes; how else can he
teach us what faith and love are? It is at such times
that we can show whether or not we trust God, even
though we are so baffled by his silence.

When I conducted funerals in my early days as a

pastor I sometimes read out Psalm 23 as though it referred to actual death. But the phrase 'the valley of the shadow of death' has nothing to do with physical death. Instead, it is a picture of the narrow, dark ravine which the shepherd sometimes had to lead his flock through in order to get to the better pasture. Snakes slithered there; thorny branches overhung, mire bogged him down, and sometimes wild beasts attacked. When traversing the valley the sheep had to trust the shepherd blindly, for he was at the front, leading them through it. The sheep might not have heard his voice often, but he was there. So when we are going through these dark and silent times, we have to remember consciously that our Shepherd is not far away. He has not forgotten us at all.

In our last year in Liverpool we had experienced great satisfaction, for the ministry was still quite fruitful. During our ten years there, several sick people were healed, many souls saved, and some cases of acute depression dealt with. Whole families were among the saved, and the church had flourished. But there was also a great deal of sorrow and frustration during this period. Sometimes we cried out 'Praise the Lord' and at others, 'Where are you, Lord?' There were times when we felt pangs something like those of the bereaved, who having heard a beloved voice often, suddenly hear that dear voice no more. Few things on earth are so desolating. It is even more desolating when that dear missing voice is that of God. No wonder the psalmist likens these pangs to those of hell when he cries out 'Do not be deaf to me, lest, if thou be silent to me, I become like those who go down to the pit.' The scriptures which tell of his love and care for us are almost a form of torment at such times. We know they are true, but we cry out 'Where, O where is he? Why is he so silent? He is supposed to be our Father. We would not treat our sons and daughters like this— where then is his fatherliness?'

And yet, God *is* faithful; he is not more loving in the light than in the dark. He is just as caring, though he says not a word. We knew these truths, but now we had to prove them in greater measure. We were in good company!

Abraham endured twenty-five years of the silence of God after the great promise of a son to him. Moses was forty years in the desert, in which time—as far as we can gather—God said little. In their cases, God was silent because he was teaching them faith and endurance, not punishing them for their sins. There were indeed times like this in the history of Israel when the 'word from the Lord was rare in those days' (1 Sam 3:1). These were times when God was disciplining his people because of their negligence and sin. It's important, then, to find out the reason for God's silence. On the one hand, we mustn't hunt perpetually to see if there is yet more sin in our lives, for we'll always find something in which we fall short of God's standards. On the other hand, we must keep short accounts with him so that he does not have to withdraw the sense of his presence from us as a punishment.

Habakkuk, even though he fasted, prayed and waited on God for a long time, heard nothing and cried out 'How long O Lord will I call for help, and thou wilt not hear?' (Hab 1:2). Amos wrote about 'not a famine for bread or a thirst for water, but rather for hearing the words of the Lord' (Amos 8:11). But, after all, why should God have spoken any more to a nation which ignored his word continually?

So it is not unusual for us in our day to pass through times when God says very little. His reason for silence is the same old reason he has always had—that we may trust him more; that we may spend more time in the earnest seeking of his face; to strengthen faith, and to show the hosts above that he knew what he was doing when he brought mankind into his family. God is saying to them, 'You watch, even though I am silent, they will still love and trust me.' Sometimes the Enemy impedes the word of God; his armies get in the way of the angels who often bring God's word to us. In addition spiritual deafness prevents us from hearing the word of God; obviously sin will block our ears to his voice. So, we had to consider all these things in this period, and we had to learn through it. We did indeed learn, and it was well worth it.

The pangs of separation

I began to travel far afield, much to my amazement; I am not a traveller by nature, and I hated the separation from my wife and family. It was in fact one of the hardest things God asked me to bear. In my times of misery, especially when pain and deafness took over and I was stuck in lonely hotels, I found it necessary to put my 'sufferings' alongside those of Jesus. Of course, they paled into insignificance.

Being absent during the children's more formative years was a trial for me, but the greatest strain came on to Peggy, who had to be mother and father to them. God gave her great grace and wisdom, which, added to her great grit, enabled Peggy to bring up our children in the fear and admonition of the Lord. She was still in pain or discomfort, and my knowledge

of her pain made it agonising to leave her and go
preaching elsewhere.

Our three children found things trying, too. They
were all Christians, and Ruth and Mark were by now
old enough to think for themselves about divine
healing. They both believed that God could heal the
sick, but their faith was shaken because he did not
respond with a 'yes' to their heartfelt prayers for their
beloved mum and dad. Andrew, the youngest, hadn't
quite worked out his healing theology, and was much
shielded by his big sister anyway. Ruth felt surges of
anger, as did Mark; not against God, but the devil.
They expressed their frustration to God and cried
out to him to do something. Mark said, 'Lord, if I
were able to heal like you, I would never hold it back.
Why do you?' Ruth got quite angry when Christians
came to visit but merely quoted proof texts to us
instead of bringing healing. Fear came in to the
hearts of both the older children. They wondered
what would happen if we died. Whenever Ruth had
any mysterious pains, she wondered if it was the onset
of her mother's disease. Andrew wondered if he
would see us in heaven, and if not, whether there was
anywhere else to go. Despite all the trauma, they all
say that life was pretty rich. Andrew says, 'Our family
life broadened our horizons and expanded our minds.
Because Dad's work enabled him to take holidays to fit
in with school breaks, we were able to go all over the
place together and mix with many people.'

We had plenty of family fun. Because Peggy could
not stand without wobbling, for example, it was
rather hard for her to berate the children when they
misbehaved, while still retaining her dignity and
authority. Every time she wagged her finger at them,
she would slowly lose her balance and head for the

floor. She therefore developed the habit of hanging on to the large handle on the fridge door, and from that safe place she would discipline the children. So when she was near that door looking around in an authoritative manner, one or other of the children would shout, 'Mother is by the fridge.' They would then come and kneel at her feet crying out, 'Mum, whatever we've done, we are sorry.' Usually, everyone dissolved into laughter, which prevented undue tension, too. Humour does help prevent self-pity and self-absorption.

Andrew says that his parents' sickness helped him to be more thoughtful and made him anticipate the things Peggy would need when I was away. He also did the shopping, perhaps one reason why he is successful in business today! My frequent absences brought an identity crisis for him. Having to depend so heavily on his mother during these trips, he wondered who this man was when I came home, but as he says, 'Because Dad prayed so much for us, it did not cause any lasting trouble, and I saw that God requires sacrifice from his servants. Mum and Dad were no exception. God did not leave us while Dad was away, and he gave us the grace of readjustment when he returned.'

I freely confess that while I was away on ministry trips, and after the meetings were over, I would often cry myself to sleep. It was often a real tussle between my desire to be a 'normal' husband and father, and the clear command of God to preach and teach all over the place. The attitude of some Christians added to the pain in that they used to hint that it was the mark of an uncaring husband to leave a sick wife while I fulfilled myself and pursued my own career. It was in this period that all my previous consecration was put to the test. Love for God can be mere words unless our right reactions prove otherwise. How good it is when we can honestly say, a bit like Paul, that 'the love of Christ controls [constrains] us' (2 Cor 5:14).

Visions

One of the greatest blessings which God gave me, and which helped me to bash on in the work during these difficult days, as well as to fuel the fires of my love for him, were some wonderful visions. Such things are never given as pure luxuries, they are always for a purpose, and those he gave me served a great purpose. One was a vision of the entry into heaven of those who have pressed on with God despite the pressures which come with it. I was among them, to my great joy and relief. A great angel blew a trumpet and announced the name of each person newly arriving there. Many other angels came to welcome and attend them as God's royal ones. Jesus himself received them, introducing them to his Father with great joy. Jesus then said, 'Let the attendants bring the rewards stored up for this child of God.' Wonderful angels, including those who had a special task to protect them on earth, brought the piles of rewards to the throne. This pile seemed to include diadems, title deeds, and sceptres, but I was not too sure about this. I knelt before Jesus and said to him, 'Lord, you gave me these rewards for my faithfulness on the earth; now it is my great privilege to offer them back to you as an act of worship.' Every time I or one of the others did this, all heaven's hosts erupted in a great outburst of wonder, love and praise. Looking at God, I could see the expression of utter love and appreciation on his face. This vision moved me to tears of gratitude and gave me the will to press on; it is so worthwhile to do so.

I know perfectly well that no one has ever seen the full glory of God, and I do not pretend that I have; but the visions are glorious and life-changing.

Another vision which helped me whenever I tended to grumble at the suffering involved in our life and ministry was that of Calvary from different standpoints. Jesus was stretched out on the cross, the loneliest place ever known, but the Holy Spirit was still with him, enabling him to fulfil the purpose of God. Jesus was looking upwards at the Father, who showed thorough approval of the sheer obedience of his Son. Then the scene changed; the Father's face darkened with holy anger and he began to turn it away from Jesus. At the same time the great doors of heaven were slowly being shut. Looking down now at the cross, I saw the face of Christ becoming dreadfully ugly, horrible and repulsive. The Holy Spirit began to withdraw from the One who had never grieved him, and Jesus was terribly alone. The communion between Father and Son was breaking down because human sin, for which he was the scapegoat, was coming between them. Darkness was falling, and then the Father turned his face completely from Jesus, and heaven's great doors were slammed shut. It was at that moment that Jesus screamed out in excruciating agony, 'My God, why hast thou forsaken me?' The effect on me ever since this vision has been profound. It makes all my troubles seem so small, and it makes me rise up in new devotion, to get on with the work.

I found that God was developing the prophetic aspect of the ministry he had given me as I travelled. And yet, despite the many revelations of Christ, and those revelations about the situation of others, God did not show us anything about our own physical condition. Cry as we might, the heavens were like brass for us. One healing meeting after another produced nothing for us except sentimental prayers, and prophecies spoken largely out of sincere optimism. Still, wherever I travelled the heavens were open, and revelation about others was quite clear. Our cry was 'O Lord, where are you? You speak concerning others, why don't you speak about us?' Psalm 28:1 became almost a liturgy to me: 'My rock, do not be deaf to me, lest, if thou be silent to me I become like those who go down to the pit. Hear the voice of my supplications when I cry to thee for help.' I became obsessed with the need to hear his voice speaking about our healing—so much so that my ministry to others became something of a formality. Our need was as great as theirs, I reasoned, so why should I bother too much with them? But when God calls us to minister to others, he gives the grace needed to be unselfish. After a while I realised I was becoming self-absorbed and thus unlike the Master.

I realised, too, that my fasting for our healing was becoming a hunger strike, to which God never responds. So, baffled and bewildered though we were at the time—unsure whether he was saying 'no' or 'wait'—we decided that if God was not answering us in this matter, we had better get on with the things about which he was speaking to us. At least God's silence and delay resulted in his enjoying more fellowship with us as we sought him day after day. Perhaps this is one main reason why he does it!

6

Our God Reigns

It is one thing to sing this song, but quite another to believe its truth when all the evidence seems to say that he does not reign.

It was in 1974 that we moved to York. Our friends Harvey and Valerie Dean attended St Cuthbert's Church (later transferred to St Michael-le-Belfrey Church), and, seeing that we have never been tied to a denomination, we went along there, too. We had no thoughts whatsoever of being in any position of responsibility, though after a while the vicar asked me to be an elder (these were early days for Anglican elders), even though I refused to become an Anglican. So because I felt sure that God was in the matter, I became an elder there. Credit is due to the vicar and the Archbishop of York, who were gracious in allowing me to minister in the church despite my nonconformity. Frequent travels precluded attendance at all elders' meetings, but I brought prophecy from time to time, both to them, and to the church, as God enabled. Group leadership and teaching in the prayer and Bible study meetings was a great joy to us, and we

learned a great deal in that church. Our children
were blessed in the youth group and matured con-
siderably in those formative years.

Wavering in faith

When God allows stronger testing, most of us scream;
if we keep on screaming he may decrease the pressure, but can we then fulfil our destiny? Isn't it better
to persevere under pressure? It's easy to sing 'Follow,
follow. I will follow Jesus, anywhere, everywhere, I
will follow on,'[1] but far from easy to practise it; it is
much easier to waver in faith and obedience.

Wavering is nothing new; it can be seen in Scripture, where far greater people than we are have
wavered. Elijah, that rugged prophet who demolished the prophets of Baal, turned the course of a
nation, put the fear of God into ungodly King Ahab,
withstood fearsome Queen Jezebel, manifested the
power and anger of the great God Jehovah, then
wavered when the evil queen threatened his life. Let's
be fair to Elijah; he had used up all his energy; he had
concentrated totally on his work for a long period;
and had just run twenty miles, much of it uphill. So
he was tired! Still the nation to whom he spoke was a
nation of waverers, and though (or perhaps because)
he was one of them, he said to them, 'How long will
you hesitate between two opinions?' The Israelites in
the wilderness wavered when the supplies ran low.
(Just like most of us!) Peter wavered as he walked
across the water and looked down at the waves.
Martha and Mary wavered when they saw their

---

[1] CSSM Songbook. Author unknown.

brother dying, and certainly wavered when he had been dead four days. The disciples wavered when they saw that Jesus' methods of establishing the kingdom—despite the Romans—did not involve weapons.

He must be Lord, but . . .

Our own faith wavered, especially when Peggy's condition grew worse, until she was not able to walk unassisted. Much prayer went up from some of the loving people in the church, but to no apparent avail. Our situation was nowhere near as difficult as some we know of, but we did need help. Eventually it came partly through our own dear children. Their love, sensitivity and humour helped us enormously in our difficulties. Even though they found life especially trying at this time, they coped wonderfully well. God was moulding our children as well as us through our situation.

After much thought and anguish of heart, we bought an electric vehicle to enable Peggy to get around without me as a 'minder'. Our anguish had stemmed from our mental conflict: a desire to see a miracle of healing, which never came, and the need to do something to help Peggy meanwhile. We reasoned thus: 'If Jesus is really Lord, he can heal . . . If we buy this buggy, it could be a lack of faith . . . But God gives us commonsense . . . Yes, but that can be an enemy of faith . . . But God has not told us not to buy it . . . Ah, but perhaps you are not seeking him earnestly enough—if you did, you would hear him. But Jesus *is* Lord, and he is an understanding Lord. He is not hard and fast. He is in control; all things *do* work for our good. Now if he is in control, and does not heal, he has decided not to heal. For if he intended to, he would have done so by now . . . Ah yes, but it may not be his time. Well, at this rate we'll be healed just barely before we die . . . Now that is the voice of unbelief . . . Indeed it is,' we cried, 'but O Lord, I believe, help my unbelief.'

Peggy, with her active mind, found many things hurtful, for example to think that she might die before the children grew up. Her prayer was 'O Lord, please let me survive until the children grow up.' This unselfish attitude is typical of her, and, thank God, her prayer has been answered in that our children are now grown up and committed to loving and serving God.

While the debates raged on in us, we still had battered leaders coming to us, needing to be looked after; we had to reach out to them, binding their wounds, comforting them in their sorrows, and healing their hurts. Few of them guessed at our own sorrow and hurts. We did not see much point in sharing them with these folk—they were understandably absorbed in their own troubles.

'Thou shalt bash on'

Once I was speaking at a conference during a time of pressure and difficulty. My subject was perseverance. As I spoke, the words quoted above came to me—and have helped me ever since. I hear them quoted all over the country, so they might have been inspired!

Whether our circumstances are hurtful or not, the Bible declares that Jesus is Lord, and we believe that he is Lord. But where, O where, was the evidence? It was at such times that we had to repeat the word in our hearts, 'Jesus is Lord . . .' At the same time, however, I privately added, 'I think!'

Eventually we have to make a choice, either to sink into unbelief, or to press on and declare publicly and privately—to mankind and to devils—that he is Lord, proofs or not. After all, the Bible declares that even 'if we are faithless, he remains faithful, for he cannot deny himself' (2 Tim 2:13).

The struggle in our hearts about whether the lordship of Christ really did extend over all circumstances lasted a long time. We found ourselves in the same position as many people in the Bible. David, although the appointed king, still had to hide in caves, was pursued by an enraged King Saul, was despised by many, deprived of a home and its comforts . . . yet God *had* made him king. Where was this vindicating God?

Hosea must have wondered where the lordship of God was in his grievous circumstances. Told by the God he loved to marry a harlot, to bring up children who might or might not have been his, laughed at by those who saw him cuckolded time after time, yet all this time he must carry on his priestly ministry without being obviously vindicated by God.

Stephen the martyr must have wondered why God did not save him from the mob, since God could do anything. The other martyrs of Bible times, and even those in the Russian gulags today, must have wondered where the almighty power of God had got to in their times of desperate need and trouble.

Martha and Mary believed that Jesus was Lord, but where, O where, was the proof of it? All they could see for a while was the dead body of their beloved brother.

The disciples in Gethsemane saw their mighty Lord pinioned by man and taken away to death. This Jesus, the mighty Son of God, was flogged at will by cruel soldiers; but no angels came to help; God did not intervene from heaven. Why? And where was this God who was supposed to be in control? 'God reigns' sounds hollow sometimes. 'Injustice reigns' seems more like the truth.

Yet why should God intervene in life? If we insist that he should, then we must expect constant intervention, correction, and even the frustrating of what we want to do. If God is expected to intervene once, then he must have the right to do so all the time.

If beauty of character is God's main objective in our lives, then we must see sickness and testing as opportunities, not obstacles. Sickness need not render a Christian useless in the holy war; in fact it can increase his usefulness to the commander. A sick Christian who fights on shows the character which God looks for—God's SAS, so to speak; His 'quick response unit' is usually made up of those who refuse to whine when the going is tough. Perhaps God deliberately allows tough trials in order to sort out the men from the boys, and the women from the girls! The word 'tribulation' is from the Latin *tribulum*, a Roman threshing instrument used to separate the grain from the chaff. Those who wielded this fearsome thing were not noted for 'mercy', rather for the vigour in which they wielded it. But they did pile up grain. Someone wrote, 'If Jesus is not Lord of all, he is not Lord at all.' There is truth in this, but how will it be shown if his lordship in our lives is not tested? And what better test than trial and trouble? If he is truly Lord of our heart during such stress, then he really is Lord.

Our refuge at these times has been the presence of God. We understand what the Psalmist was saying in Psalm 73:16–17: 'When I pondered to understand this, it was troublesome in my sight until I came into the sanctuary of God,' and Psalm 63:2 adds 'To see thy power and glory.' A sight of God is a life saver!

Functioning under pressure

A further complication in this period was that—whereas before I had simply travelled around preaching and prophesying as God showed—I now became aware of a fear in my heart of failing to live up to people's expectations of me as a godly man who manifested the power of God in my ministry. This fear led to that awful pressure to 'produce', which has killed not a few preachers before their proper time. I found that people were looking askance at me, and I read their thoughts: 'This man is supposed to be a man of God; he preaches big things, but there is not much sign of them; Brother X has more results than he does; anyway, what about his sick wife?'

I began to refrain from preaching too much about a great God in case he asked me to minister to the sick. But it led to torment in my heart because I knew that God was all-powerful. In fact I had seen two miracles of healing in Africa, and quite a number of healings in the UK.

It was in the late 1970s that I accompanied Denis Clark on a trip to South Africa. After we had preached together in several cities, he went on to Kenya, and I went to preach in a small town elsewhere. I thought I was going to a fairly large rally, and because there was a trace of preacher's pride in me, I looked forward to a bit of limelight. When I arrived, there were only a handful of people in the place. In the front row was a woman who was terribly crippled with arthritis. I began to speak in a desultory way, and found myself saying, 'The God I serve can do

anything.' The crippled woman said, 'Can he heal
me?' I said, 'Yes, of course'—without much conviction or interest. To my amazement, she suddenly
stood up, her bones cracking into place, and her face
lighting up with joy. She stuffed her crutches into the
pastor's hands and rushed out into the night, glorifying God. I was so amazed, shaken and ashamed that I
closed the meeting and went to my lodgings in total
confusion. God, being so merciful, brought many
people along afterwards, and there was considerable
blessing. A woman was healed of a similar health
problem at a meeting in Liverpool which had actually
been convened for prayer for revival. Again, I was
not even preaching about healing, but she stood up in
such pain and with such a heartfelt cry for help that I
went over to her and simply said, 'Be healed now, in
the great name of Jesus.' And she was!

Despite these encouraging events, my ministry
became rather mediocre as I wrestled with guilt and
fear. Amazingly enough, God still blessed me, but
only in small ways. Despair took hold of me, and I felt
a strong desire to retreat into a fatalistic position.
Then I would not have to worry because it would all
be up to God; and I could not bring the power of God
to bear, because it was all in his sovereignty!

Guilt assailed me, too, because I could do nothing
to help my dear wife in her illness, despite seeing
others healed from time to time. I began to rage
against God; he seemed indifferent to my cries on her
behalf saying, 'Lord, I tramp around serving you with
all the sacrifice involved in that kind of work; I serve
you faithfully in this ministry; I pray my heart out,
and yet you do nothing for me.'

Time after time the Enemy whispered 'You are a
hypocrite; you preach these great things, but you

don't believe them. And in any case he doesn't listen to you. Nor does he vindicate your work. You may as well pack up and go back to work in industry.'

Even the word of God 'tried us', as it tried Joseph in Psalm 105:19. (At least we were in good company!) I wept often before God saying, 'O Lord, you have sworn that this Bible is true, and I believe you. But Lord, how long before I see it proved before my eyes?' I began to loathe testimonies. They were all about events 'over there' or 'there', whereas I was aching for them to be seen *here*. And yet I could not doubt some of the testimonies, and I tried hard to rejoice with the people who had been healed. But I must confess that it was—and still is at times—a gritted teeth job!

But *our God reigns. And that is gloriously true!* Although we have shared our hearts very honestly in this book, and revealed some of our frustrations and fears, I hope that the many joyful times and the very many blessings are clear too. God is good, and we know it, despite all the delays, silences, and pains which we have known. The celestial city beckons, and we are on our way there. Hallelujah!

7

Our Enemy

During 1980 I had been wondering for some time if God was putting me back into the pastoral ministry, and several friends had indicated the same thing. Although there were blessings in the travelling ministry, it was also an increasing strain. I have to admit, too, that my dislike of travelling was a factor in my thinking.

At the end of that year I realised that our work in the church at York was finished. So the question arose: 'Where do we go from here?' Even though I still believed our maturity was sufficient for God to say that we could move anywhere we wanted to, we felt the need of specific guidance this time. We sought God earnestly for definite leading, but again no answer came. I decided to move anyway.

I feel now, looking back, that I made the mistake of looking for a convenient place to go rather than waiting until God was pleased to show us clearly where he wanted us to go. Peggy was not keen to move, and I should have taken more notice of her reluctance. However, a man we had known for some years came to see me, and he offered me the chance to be a co-pastor in Dunstable. Thinking that this would enable me to combine the settled and the travelling ministry, it seemed a good idea.

At the time, we were carrying heavy responsibilities: we were part of the Spring Harvest team; working in and eventually leading Intercessors for Britain and the Prayer and Bible Weeks, plus being among the leaders of Intercessors International; helping with the Bible Meditation courses; serving numerous churches . . . and so on. We therefore needed the help, love and support of a local fellowship, and we were convinced we would be able to find them at Dunstable.

We moved there in 1980. Life was complicated again because my facial paralysis had got worse, and in fact my mouth was nearly round to my ear when I smiled. Not only was this painful, but it was also extremely embarrassing on public platforms. A godly surgeon, Edward Short, arranged then for me to have a facelift. It has helped me a lot, although I still cannot close one eye properly. (However, that is a great help in watching while praying!)

As we got our house ready for occupation, thanks to the tremendous help of the people in the church, our travels were necessarily curtailed for a while. Because I preached a lot in the church while the pastor took a sabbatical break, and because of added pastoral responsibilities, our presence there was essential, although we still travelled to some extent, and even more so when the pastor came back after his break.

The battlefield

As a rule, it is not too long after we become Christians that we realise we have a fight on our hands. Our Enemy proves to be adept at leading us into sin, even though we love the Lord and want to serve him well. Satan has had centuries of experience in seducing mankind, and drawing him away from the paths of righteousness. We must therefore have a realistic view of the devil's power if we are to combat him. He is not all-powerful—only God is—but we must have a healthy respect for his abilities. We do not need to be afraid of him, for he is a defeated foe, but we cannot afford to be cheeky or careless in our warfare against him. He cannot be everywhere at once, for only God has that ability. Nor can he know everything. Jesus destroyed his power, and Jesus gives his own victory and authority to us to make us triumphant.

Most of the conferences where I ministered were called together for spiritual warfare, and it was in them that I learned most about the activities of God's Enemy, the devil, and how to combat them. For a while we made the mistake of thinking that spiritual warfare consisted only of strong prayer, but we saw later that evangelism and holy living were aspects of it as well (salt is the enemy of corruption, and light of darkness). Obviously, those who are heavily involved in this warfare are prime targets for counter-attacks from the evil one, and we were no exception. We were, and still are, attacked; but as long as we truly love the Lord, we count it worthwhile to be involved in his war, for his sake.

Satan's weapons

The devil attacks mankind in many ways: by pushing people into alcohol and drug abuse; sexual immorality; the love of money with all the corruption that brings; the occult; pride and power seeking. He also attacks our bodies through sickness, and will even murder us by any means if he can manage it. Yet one of his main targets is the mind.

Battle for the mind

Peggy writes at length here about the battle for our minds:

'The human mind is a wonderful and complex thing; to be able to understand, think, and plan, to name only some of its attributes makes me very grateful for such ability. We are made in God's image, and as Christians we can say, "We have the mind of Christ." It is therefore not surprising that the mind is a battleground for the devil. Christians do not escape his devious and troubling attacks. He cannot take away our salvation, but he tries to take away our peace and keep us in mental torment: bewildered and ineffective.

'When Jesus went into the wilderness after he had been baptised in the Spirit, he had just been affirmed by God as his beloved Son. It was not necessary to add the term "beloved", but because God is so generous and abundant in his approval of his Son, he wholeheartedly affirmed him. When after forty days' fasting Jesus was feeling the discomfort of hunger, the devil—typically—attacked him on a fundamental point saying, "If you are the Son of God. . . ."

'It is not surprising that he attacks us when we are discomforted. In my case he attacks me when I recall the time when I could run and walk, or at least climb on to a stool, not to mention when I could climb hills. I cannot help these thoughts coming, but as someone said "You cannot stop the birds from flying over your head, but you can stop them from making a nest in your hair." Scripture says, "Forgetting those things which are behind, and pressing towards the mark . . . ."

'My thoughts cause me pain, but I work it out in daily living by calling out to the Lord, and then turning to other more helpful thoughts. It does not help to dwell on my disability, although the past does not need to be a "no-go area". Not all my memories are of my ability or lack of it. The devil wants me to dwell on the negative, but the verses in Romans 8:28–29 encourage me to anchor all my thoughts on Jesus, and to trust him. He knows all about me and loves me, though his is not a sentimental love. God called Jesus the Beloved, but still allowed him to suffer. And he has plans for my future, as well as caring for me now, for I am beloved of God, too.

'The verses in Romans say, "All things work together for good to those who love God, and are called according to his purpose." Having established that we love him and are called by him, we can put all our trust on this verse. "All" means all, and "good" means good. However, this verse is incomplete without the following verse which says, "We are predestined to be moulded in to the image of his Son." In other words, we are to be made Christlike. I cannot say that I understand every aspect of my own condition, but I do find peace in these verses, for God is making me Christlike, and so I trust him to do it.

'Having said that, I balance another truth in tension with the above, Psalm 103: ". . . who forgives all your sins, and heals all your diseases." As a Christian I want *all* that Jesus died on the cross to bring to me. He enabled God to forgive my sin, and I am looking to him for the healing made possible by his triumph there.

'We belong to a "me-centred" generation, and its beliefs feed the humanistic approach. God however longs for a God-centred generation, and for God-centred Christians. The Westminster Catechism says, "Man's chief end is to glorify God, and to enjoy Him for ever." I have learned so much of God myself, and if I can keep my focus on him, then I will please him and enjoy him even if I am not healed, but I cannot ignore my desire for wholeness too.'

Like Peggy, I've discovered that Satan will go to any lengths to affect the mind, and he uses many weapons to do so. Today he even uses the information over-load to which the press, TV and junkmail subject us all. More than one person known to me has succumbed to that pressure and has finished up in a mental hospital. The pressure of advertising has pushed many young people into sins such as immorality and covetousness. Some, though not all, in the media have a lot to answer for when they stand before God, as they must in the Day of the Lord.

Satan loves to sow confusion in our minds. Doubt, fear, and discouragement are favourite weapons for this purpose. He also loves to bring us down through constant accusation, for Jesus said that he is the 'accuser' (one who speaks us down, a denigrator). If he can introduce any of these repeated accusations into our minds, he can ruin our whole lives. He managed it at the dawn of creation with Adam and Eve. Initially their minds were at rest because God had given them clear instructions about what they could and could not do. They rejoiced to follow his wise counsel. But Satan came to attack them, and his first assault was on their minds. He set out to instil in them the desire to be like God, ie, all-knowing and powerful. He wanted them to be independent and self-confident, feeling no need of God. So he whispered, 'Has God said . . . ?' He still whispers it today.

His strategy takes many forms. He sometimes tries to magnify things in our lives out of proportion—marriage tensions, the possibility of redundancy, minor quarrels, and the like—and thus to divert us from the purpose of God. He will try to get us to focus on our immediate circumstances rather than the eternal future; on our welfare and satisfaction here and now, rather than the greater life above. This is how he builds his strongholds in man's mind. Some of these are discussed below.

Disappointment and discouragement

One of his most potent weapons against Peggy has been disappointment. Having had several prophecies that God would heal her physically, she watched and waited day after day for their fulfilment. In a church newly stirred by the Holy Spirit, a sincere Christian lady suddenly laid hands on her and prayed for her healing. Again Peggy waited and hoped for evidence of it. When it did not come, she felt guilty, thinking it must be due to a fault in her; or that the woman had faith, but she did not. After several episodes like this, she hardly expected anything to happen, so then she was not surprised when nothing did. She says:

'Because in the early days I was fairly mobile and able to care for the family, though with difficulty, I just got on with living and concluded that the prophecies must be true but would only happen in God's good time. Life went on, and periodically I would think, "Perhaps this is the time for healing." But so

far that time hasn't come. After many disap-
pointments it is easy to become bitter, but I'm grateful
to God that I'm not. I have suffered, been deeply
disappointed and hurt, but I love God, trust him, and
I know that he is good. This does not mean that I am
never sad or bewildered, but I know that the best
thing for me is to get closer to God and to know him
better. This I seek to do by talking often to him and
by constant meditation in his word. I do not understand all God's ways, but I know he loves me. He has a
purpose and a plan for my life and is working on me,
for me, and through me. Therefore, when I speak—
publicly or privately—I believe people realise that I
do not speak lightly, but from conviction and
experience.'

Doubt

Peggy and I found that Satan's attacks on our minds
increased even more as we pressed on with the work
he gave us to do. To some degree he succeeded in
putting serious doubts into our minds for a while,
although God gave us victory over them eventually.
These attacks initially resulted in a crisis of confidence; mostly of confidence in God, but also in
ourselves. We asked ourselves, 'Does God intend to
heal us physically, or not?' Despite much reading of
Scripture, our doubt persisted, and there were times
when I could hear an audible voice jeering at me and
saying that all healing finished with the apostles. (I am
quite sure now that this was the voice of Satan.)

We spent time trying to find out if there was any
hidden sin in our lives. The trouble is with such
explorations that we can always find something
wrong, and the Enemy is good at keeping our eyes on
such things. For a while, he succeeded. Then he

would assail us with the thought that God would only heal us if we were almost perfect and free from sin. So what hope was there for us? Periodically it seemed that there was none.

The fiercest battles were those in which our circumstances seemed to contradict the word of God. The Bible said that God was loving, and that he is 'the Lord who heals us'; but our affairs seemed to say that he was not. We shared the same thoughts that assail all human beings at different times; we asked, 'Why does a good God allow the righteous to suffer, and the wicked to get away with murder?'

Later, the questions in our minds changed, and we began to wonder if we were really in the will of God or not. Had we been right in our various moves, or had we gone out of God's will in going to the various places? If so, could we ever go back and start again? Satan made many other attacks, but we have included the above examples simply to make the point that the devil aims at the mind. We do want to stress in other chapters of this book, however, that there is a defence against them—and that it works! Ephesians 6:16 says, 'In addition to all, [take] up the shield of faith with which you will be able to extinguish all the flaming missiles of the evil one.' Here are more of these missiles.

Unbelief

Unbelief is the twin of doubt; one works with the other. Let doubt linger, and it will call in unbelief to compound the problem. We may not forsake our preaching, but it will be shot through with unreality. We may pay great attention to the letter of Scripture, but it will become cerebral, and our preaching will lack results.

God mercifully helped us in our troubles, largely through the Scripture embedded in us through Bible meditation. (See my book *Bible Meditation*.) Like Jesus, we learned more about the art of resisting the devil with the Bible, both by quoting it at him, and by filling our minds with it. This practice left little room for doubt. Whether we win this battle for the mind depends quite largely on what we fill it with. If we obey the injunction in Philippians 4:8 and fill our minds with those things which are 'true, honourable, right, pure, lovely, and of good repute . . .', then we will have strong defences against the Enemy's assaults upon us. Peggy and I obeyed this scripture, and thus found God's help. The love of good and godly friends helped us, too. They were the sort of friends who knew better than to butter us with mere optimism.

Fear

The Bible says that Satan fires 'missiles' at us, and that he builds fortresses in our minds if he can. I believe that some of the 'fortresses' mentioned in 2 Corinthians 10:4–5 were erected, and had to be demolished, in our own minds. There was the stronghold of anticipatory fear, one of the devil's best weapons. Peggy would start to wonder what would happen if she could not move at all, or if her internal organs stopped working properly, or if she could not run our home any more. I would wonder how we would manage if my remaining 10% hearing were to disintegrate, leaving me stone deaf. How would I preach, and if I could not do so, would that be the end of my ministry? How would we live? What if Peggy died? If I died first, how would she cope? For a while, these and many other fears gripped us and left us quite shattered.

The way to deal with fear is first to realise that it is actually sin: unbelief and disobedience combined. If God says so often in the Bible that we should 'fear not', we either respond in faith and turn away from it; or we do not respond, and remain a victim of fear.

There is a difference between fear and a nervous temperament. We may have been born with a timid nature, and this is not our fault, though we still need to cope with it. But fear comes when we allow that which threatens us to gain entry into our minds. We are listening then to the devil's temptations and succumbing to them, instead of hearing and believing the plain word of God. That turns temptation into sin. But if we hear God and take hold of his hand, turning away from fear, then we have dealt with it; our life and ministry are no longer paralysed.

Bitterness

If we allow the devil to persuade us to dwell on the apparent injustice of our circumstances, especially if we contrast our supposed uprightness with the more obviously sinful behaviour of others who are well and strong, then he is likely to erect a stronghold of bitterness in our minds. Peggy has never felt bitter, but I must confess that I have. For a time I could barely look at healthy Christians without feeling bitter. To this day I do not know how God still blessed my ministry while I was so horrible inside.

Grace is the answer. That is why things are different now. All through this book we are recounting things which we have passed through and triumphed over. We are saying that it is possible to overcome all these crippling spiritual 'diseases' if we truly want to. And we do!

So many of God's people are disqualified from

God's service because they harbour bitterness. Their festering spirit not only disqualifies them from usefulness, but it also damages those around them. The writer of Hebrews 12:15 warns us in no uncertain terms that we can defile the body of Christ by holding on to grudges and to all the things which produce this corrosive poison. 'See to it that no one comes short of the grace of God, that no root of bitterness springing up causes trouble, and by it many be defiled.' I have seen churches come to a halt in their ministry because some of their members have been bitter against each other. Who says we can sin in private? Sin's results affect the whole body. Is there a remedy? Yes. The grace of God, freely available to all who decide they need it, and want it, and come to him for it. Then let's use it!

Cynicism

Bitterness also has a twin: cynicism. This is a constant danger to those who are frustrated in their search for spiritual reality. There are so many stories; so many 'healed' backs, which really owe their healing to pain-killing drugs. Glowing testimonies to miracles which, on enquiry, prove to have disappeared overnight. Prophecies which promised much but brought little, always saying what God was going to do in the future, but producing nothing now. The laying on of hands . . . but empty hands. Great swelling prayers . . . but only sanctified verbiage. Plenty of jovial optimism . . . but no real faith. Fervent healers demanding in stentorian voices, with distended neck veins, and with fractured grammar that we 'Get up in the name o' Jesus, Hallelujah! Glory ter God—er.'

Yes, on occasions I became cynical, although Peggy did not. It was wrong of me, I confess it. Surely many testimonies are true; of course they are, thank God. How essential it is to dwell on those things which are true, and put up with those which are sadly untrue. If we dwell on the negative all the time, we become negative ourselves, and negativity soon degenerates into cynicism. We could not avoid the questions arising in our minds (Where, O where is God? Will he heal, or won't he?)—but at least we avoided the trap of cynicism. I say again, however, that it was by holding to the word of God. Only when we *use* Scripture will we destroy these strongholds of the devil in our minds.

Yet another phase

At the beginning of 1982, Denis Clark, the founder and leader of Intercessors for Britain, died. As a result, I needed to make changes in my own life. I had become close to Denis, and he was the one who first opened the way for the prophetic ministry God had given me. I asked many godly people to pray about the new leadership of IFB and the prayer and Bible weeks. This time I was super careful! The more they prayed, and the more I prayed, the more sure we all felt that God was telling me to take over both these ministries. I did not really want to do so, nor did I feel capable of handling them. In the end, however, I felt that God gave me no option, so I took it over. I was very much aware that it would be a caretaker operation until either it was time for the prayer and Bible weeks and Intercessors for Britain to close down, or for me to hand over to another leader. It is always difficult to follow a giant, and particularly to satisfy his followers, but I had no intention of trying to be a Denis, and I declared that I would lead as God showed me. So I did.

Looking back now on the years 1980 to 1983, especially to the time before Denis died, I can now see that God was working far more than I could see then. The prayer and Bible weeks were strong and productive—the main platform for my ministry. I felt safe in the company of Denis Clark who had the apostolic type of ministry which complemented and guarded mine. In my moments of despair, he supported me and urged me on more than anyone else ever did. I honour his memory still, and my grief is that his great work is not more often spoken of or appreciated by so many to whom he was a father and mentor.

Eventually it became clear that I could not remain as a co-pastor and still fulfil this large work with IFB. Dunstable was not a suitable base for such a ministry; we needed to move again. It is always difficult to explain adequately to others without causing misunderstanding the reasons for moving. I will simply say, therefore, that God gave us freedom to move on, and we did so—to Chester.

8

In the Arena

Our time in Chester, from 1982 to 1987, proved to be a mixture: a massive review of our life and ministry; also a time of readjustment, sifting of motives, enjoyment, and a degree of renewal. All this, plus a heavy programme of ministry for much of the time.

Having been deeply wounded by treachery from Christian brothers whom I had previously trusted, and having been rejected by some of those to whom God brought the prophetic word through me, vilified as a 'false prophet' by some who were determined to damage my ministry, and bruised by power-hungry people—I was not in great shape for a while! I struggled hard against a descent into bitterness, and against a tremendous desire to justify myself. Mercifully, during the later stages of our time in Chester, there was a lull in invitations to minister which enabled me to pray more. I began to consider the question of the 'arena'.

Where is the arena?

As I went along the canal bank during one of my prayer walks, I recalled part of the Catechism that I learned years before, when I was a Scout. Part of it says, 'Man's chief end is to glorify God, and to enjoy him forever.' But I found myself asking, '*Where* are we to glorify God? *Where* are we to enjoy him?' One answer is this: in the arena of this present age—in Chester, London, Windsor, Bognor Regis, or where we live.

One of the verses which has made sense to us in our own experience of testing and frustration is Ephesians 3:10: '... in order that the manifold wisdom of God might now be made known through the church [Christians] to the rulers and authorities in the heavenly places'. This 'manifold wisdom' is seen first in God's choice of us, weak and foolish though we were, and still are. Because we are weak, we need all the strength God can give us. He knew this need, and he also knew that he would give it to us. Thus the heavenly powers see how wise he was to undertake this work in the first place. God's wisdom is seen, too, in the demonstration of real love and faith which we make when we react rightly in our trials and tribulations. All this takes place in the arena of our lives as we live in this world. What a privilege it is to make such a demonstration! Knowing all this activity is going on is what makes our sufferings here on earth more bearable.

We have opportunities to glorify him on earth which we will never have in heaven. Here in the 'arena' we experience the trial of faith; but in heaven faith will be superfluous, for it will have turned to sight. Here we can trust him in sickness; but in

heaven there will be no sickness. On earth our love
for God is tested; but there it will have been proved
enough, and it remains only to live in the glow of it.
Here we are surrounded by evil powers who will try
to make us deny God; but in heaven devils are
unknown. On earth we must sometimes pass through
times when God is silent and not consciously near us;
but in heaven he will never be silent, nor separate
from us.

Who are the onlookers?

The onlookers around the arena of our lives on earth
are numerous. Hebrews 12:1 refers to 'so great a
cloud of witnesses surrounding us . . .', and I believe
that these onlookers comprise the princes and powers
of heaven, including the angels of God. Meanwhile,
the 'principalities and powers' of darkness are doubt-
less among our onlookers too. As for Christians who
have gone to heaven—I am not sure that they can see
us; or at least, if they can, they will be so absorbed
with the Lord that they will not be looking at us.

We need to realise that the earth is the arena, and
that it is a battleground. We need equally to see into
the heavenly places, from which God views
everything. Remember, he can see *everything*, whereas
the devil cannot. It seems to me that our Father often
says to us, 'Why not come up here to the heavenly
places (as we do in prayer or vision), where visibility is
good. Come and see the plans of the devil in detail;
then we can combat them together.'

From our vantage point in the heavenly places, as
we 'sit with God' in our times of prayer and contem-
plation, we will see that the prince of the power of the
air (Satan) has his princes and powers around him;

not in hell, but in the air (ie, the heavenly places). It is from there that he and his princes direct the demon spirits' campaigns against the followers of Jesus on earth.

We must also realise that the Enemy has usurped the territory belonging to God. Psalm 24:1 says, 'The earth is the Lord's and all it contains;' it does *not* rightfully belong to Satan. He also holds prisoner millions who belong really to the Lord. Centuries ago God made this plain by saying through Ezekiel 'All souls are mine' (Ezekiel 18:4). And although demon powers are working overtime trying to fill hell and denude heaven, their time is short; for the Judgement Day is coming when they will be finally imprisoned for ever. This is why their attacks are so savage and unrelenting. Theirs is a campaign of hate as they seek to wear out God's saints, to murder them, and by all means to render them paralysed, or at least inefficient.

Understanding the arena's battles

In the Brethren Assembly in Ruislip where I had grown up as a Christian, we were never taught about spiritual powers. Vague references were made to evil and the need to avoid it, but we knew nothing about spiritual warfare. Nor were we taught about the power of the Holy Spirit and his gifts. And yet God was merciful to us, because he blessed the church, and many souls were saved. (I do thank God for my time there despite the lack of some key teaching.)

It was while I was in the fellowship there that I first sensed angelic protection. I was driving a heavy lorry downhill towards a busy roundabout, and the brakes failed. I saw a flash of angel movement and cried out for help. I also caught a glimpse of evil powers and knew that this was the Enemy's attempt on my life. I felt angels wrestling the steering wheel round (no power steering in those days), and they also prevented my 30-ton load from shifting. Shortly after this incident, we were working on building the new chapel and there were only two of us to lift a heavy concrete beam upright. We were standing on a trestle which wobbled, and I became acutely aware of the Enemy's desire to kill us both. Mercifully God helped us, and it was soon in place. These two events made me think more about activities in the heavenly places, and I partly grasped the idea of the arena, but for a while busy life took over and I forgot all about it . . . till later years.

A common jibe against those who are spiritual is that 'they are so heavenly minded that they are no earthly use'. This criticism has been levelled against me, and my reply has been, 'Unless you are heavenly minded, you *cannot* be of much earthly use.' If we see events only from our earthly perspective, we are bound to get confused and unbalanced. A heavenly destiny like ours demands a heavenly perspective. This is gained as we spend time with God and his word. If we desire visions and revelations, they will be given to us. This way of life will ensure that we see things from the heavenly places as well as from the arena.

Hostile forces

We have noticed the activity of evil powers wherever we have lived. Between us Peggy and I have lived in many places; I in London, Kenton, Harrow, Ruislip, Matlock, Dorset, Dawlish; and Peggy in Buxton, Manchester, and Matlock. Together we have lived in

Matlock, Liverpool, York, Dunstable, Chester and York again. In all these places Satan has his princes and demons.

Scripture indicates that there is a hierarchy in the kingdom of darkness: 'The rulers, the powers . . . spiritual forces . . .' (Eph 6:12); 'rule, authority, power. . .'(Eph 1:22). I believe these verses refer to beings, not just concepts. Satan does not do all this dirty work himself, but uses his underlings to do it, while he superintends it. Like all big cities in the UK and elsewhere, London is overseen by great evil powers, as is Liverpool. Chester and York too are overshadowed by demons who use dead religion to oppose true Christianity, as well as other powers who use different techniques. Witchcraft and resurgent Druidism are rife in many of these areas. God's Enemy will base himself in the areas where he can exert most influence; which shows that there is a real strategy behind his evil.

Sin in the world is not only a result of human failure and nastiness, but it is also a direct result of the fall of Satan from heaven, and of his consequent success in infecting mankind. Evil is a system, well directed by a cunning genius. As a result of his work in the world, many people, including Christians, labour under the curses brought upon their families in the past, often through some family member dabbling in witchcraft and other occult practices. Of course it is possible to make too much of this kind of thing, and I deplore the present tendency, in some of the counselling going on today, to exaggerate the prevalence of the occult. But we certainly do need to be aware of its reality. Praise God there is deliverance from all the devil's devices.

On some occasions we have experienced tangible

effects of satanic activity. I have felt demons preventing me from entering certain premises, by an almost physical resistance. As it turned out, I was about to reach people who were on the verge of suicide, and the last thing the demons wanted was their deliverance from it. At other times I have known a tremendous physical pushing by evil powers, almost as though they were heaving me bodily into other premises, and afterwards found that thugs were waiting there to maim me.

Friendly forces

Although the devil is busy, God's angels are busy, too. Not only are they actively waging war against evil powers, delivering many of God's saints from harm, but they are also watching carefully as God leads and works on and with his dear people; for they are deeply interested: '. . . which things the angels desire to look into' (1 Pet 1:12).

Thank God for angels; we must not worship them, but neither must we ignore them. According to Revelation 5:13 there are 'myriads' of them, and they surely outnumber the forces of darkness. Scripture says, 'Greater is he that is in you than he who is in the world' (1 John 4:4), so I presume that there are more angels in heaven than those who were thrown down from heaven (Rev 12:9). Angels surrounded Elisha when the Israelites were under threat from the Syrians. They released Peter from prison. They spoke to Mary and the shepherds. They warned Joseph in a dream to flee. They ministered to Jesus in Gethsemane, and in the wilderness time of temptation.

They even minister to ordinary people like Peggy and me. Apart from the incidents mentioned at the beginning of this chapter, angels have preserved our lives on several other occasions, both in traffic incidents, when a tyre blew out at speed on three separate occasions, and in the sometimes dangerous work among the doss house men in Liverpool.

On one such occasion, when I worked for the Liverpool City Mission, I went to a lodging house to preach to the men, but my heart quailed when I saw in the cellar about 200 men who were mad drunk on methylated spirits, all fighting with broken bottles and chair legs. I confess that I chickened out and slunk home. But on another occasion I *did* go in to talk to them about Jesus. Although some of the men were demonised as well as being very drunk, it was wonderful to sense the presence of angels that day; I was in fact able to preach with real liberty.

I have sometimes found it difficult to distinguish between drunkenness and demonisation. However, when I learned to pray more earnestly before I went to the lodging houses, instead of simply regarding my visits as part of my job, God began to give me more sensitivity. If a man is blind drunk, he shows anger, violence, and foul-mouthed abuse; but if he is demonised as well, he shows these same things, but there is also an expression of demonic hate and cunning on his face—one of the main clues. He manifests an aura of evil too, and even a peculiar smell which is different from that of unwashed bodies.

Sometimes these men showed physical strength far greater than normal. Few of them are strong, as a rule, because of the excesses in their life. On one particular day, I spoke to two men, one of whom was demonised. One was quite responsive; but just as I was to pray for him, the other came at me with a knife. The ensuing struggle spoilt the opportunity; it also spoilt my nose

for a while! At other times I was surrounded by these
vicious characters as I sought to witness to them.
They were urged on to violence by the demons who
had taken them over, as they had given way to
alcohol.

Then, through the Mission's suicide phone line, the
Enemy has tried to wear us out in another way. Here
were people apparently crying out for help, but in
reality they were fiercely holding on to their sin. Such
people cannot be helped, and we had to learn not to
give our time. The reason I mention these incidents is
simply to point out the reality of spiritual warfare,
and to share our experiences during it. Peggy and I
have gradually grown to have a heavenly perspective,
and we believe that God has been able to show all the
powers in the heavenly places how wise he is to allow
trial and trouble in our life together, because of their
good effects as we have used his grace in order to
endure. Perhaps missionaries could tell far more
wonderful stories than these, for angels are guarding,
and helping his people as they combat this ruthless
foe all over the world.

The challenge of the arena

What is this challenge? And what are all the
onlookers, including God, looking for?

All in heaven and hell are watching the people of
God to see how they respond to him as they pass
through the arena's varying circumstances. The good
powers in heaven wait to see if God's people are
loving, patient, believing, triumphant, faithful, and if
they are holy in life—or if they react badly.

Meanwhile the Enemy looks, waits, and hopes
for a demonstration of unbelief, self-centredness,

bitterness, and impatience from God's people. He will do anything to bring about our downfall. Remember, he wins many of his victories by a series of 'pin pricks'. He desperately seeks to fix in the human heart the lie that God is uncaring, almost oblivious to the crying needs of the world he created. How Satan loves it when some of God's people turn traitor against the Lord they profess to love and serve; how keen is the Evil One to instil bitterness in the hearts of those who are sick. And how easy it is for him to succeed in those who experience frustration—'hope deferred makes the heart sick' (Prov 13:12). How he taunts them with the very Scripture in which they believe, whispering, 'Surely God is a cruel liar, promising great things for you but withholding them from you in your trouble.'

Such taunts stuck in our own hearts at one stage when, even while we were experiencing pains and struggles, people still came to us for help and counsel—and found it. Their marriage problems were sometimes solved by a simple prophetic revelation. Long-standing quarrels were resolved quickly when God gave a revelation of his heart to the one who was particularly obdurate. Heart-melting visions were conveyed to many who came to us paralysed by doubts about whether they were really saved. A number of sick people were healed, and oppressed people were delivered quite quickly. Yet the Scriptures did not seem to be fulfilled for *us*. It did not seem logical or fair! I would say, 'Lord, you give them great help from us, but why don't you help *us*? You heal others through us, but you don't heal us. Why? Why?' The Enemy did have a bit of victory then.

The greatest battle of all

Satan waited and watched Jesus at Calvary to see if he could succeed in bringing down the Son of God. Just one irritable thought would do it, if Satan could introduce it into that pure spirit. Just one doubt would poison Jesus' heart towards his Father. Just one resentful, bitter word from his lips would invalidate Calvary.

God also watched his Son for as long as he could, to see if he would persevere until the work was complete. Eventually he had to turn away because it was necessary for Jesus to experience the complete rejection and alienation from God which all sinners experience when they enter hell. This is *the* Judgement! Jesus could have been delivered if he had chosen to be; he said in Gethsemane, 'I can appeal to my Father, and he will at once put at my disposal more than twelve legions of angels' (Mt 26:53). They stood by to deliver Jesus from the Enemy and the cross. But they were never called in; Jesus did it alone. What God saw enabled him to reconcile men and women to himself. What the devil saw was the final irrevocable victory of Jesus over him and all his hosts. Satan failed! Utterly. God's plan for man's future was now accomplished. It was 'finished' once and for ever. The good angels and the great heavenly princes had a fresh demonstration of God's triumphant power through his Son.

Take it, or leave it!

We also have an opportunity to glorify God on the earth. We can either take it, or we can leave it. What a privilege it is to mount a demonstration for him on earth so that he can perhaps boast of us to his angels. Through us they can see what the love of redeemed people is like; to see his grace in action in our lives; to understand what faith really is. How else can they learn, seeing that they are created beings, and in a different realm from us? They cannot be perfect in knowledge, and they are not redeemed as we are, and do not have our experiences on earth. It is for this great demonstration that we were born—our chief purpose in life to become like Jesus; to show mankind what God is like. How sad if we replace glorifying God with our petty earthly ambitions; for if we achieve them it is but for a short while and brings us only a temporary satisfaction.

We shall glorify him in heaven, too, and in far greater ways, but let us not lose the chance to do so in our earthly arena. We shall also enjoy him in heaven; our new minds will enable us to comprehend so much more of his glory. But again I say, 'Why lose the chance to enjoy him now?' Embittered people can never do so; those who rebel against their circumstances cannot do so. Those with a deliberately sinful heart know nothing of the joy of the Lord.

God is the God of the arena, loving enough to allow us the privilege of giving a demonstration of his power and grace. But he is also determined enough to keep working on us even when we scream out for easy victories. None but overcoming Christians can satisfy the purposes of this rugged God. Certainly it is Christ who overcomes through us, but he only does so when we co-operate with him. Without him we can do nothing, but without us he will not do anything. See for example 2 Corinthians 5:20, which points out that we are ambassadors for Christ, as though God were entreating through us. 'Be reconciled to God'; also

2 Corinthians 6:1: 'And working together with him . . .' Thus God *can* do anything in his almighty power, but he has decided to work through us.

Suffering is an occupational hazard for those who would be like him. The arena is a battleground on which trophies can be won, to the glory of God. Do you wonder that God allows trial and trouble? Are these things not his way of demonstrating what he can do through the very people whom his Enemy once enslaved?

When the going gets tough, the tough get going

Peggy and I persevered in our own arena, although I once came perilously close to quitting the ministry. But then what else was there to do? What other calling could match this one? Later on I began to think that there might be an easier ministry to which I could retreat into a kind of fatalism. Then it would all be up to God, not up to me. But what kind of a demonstration would that be for the God we loved? So we pressed on. I think I became a little proud of our perseverance; I at least became quite willing to talk about our circumstances in a rather heroic way. It brought the admiring look, and the approving word. How foolish can we be!

Just as foolish is the martyr spirit. The 'poor-old-me' syndrome, otherwise known as self-pity. I fell into this trap when I found myself getting irritated over the continual interruptions in our daily life. People would always call when I did not feel like talking, or just as I was putting further gems on the word processor. The phone would always ring during times of prayer, or during *Tom and Jerry*!

Some of the interruptions were necessitated by Peggy's condition. I want to say yet again that she coped amazingly well and ran the home wonderfully; but obviously there were some things which she just could not do; she needed my help. But to my warped spirit, these and other interruptions always occurred when *I* needed to concentrate, or *I* did not want to be disturbed, etc. I reasoned that I was a prophet, not a skivvy, quite forgetting that a prophet *is* a skivvy. But a skivvy for *God*! How ruthlessly God trains his servants! And I confess I found this part of his training—learning to cope with frustration, and adopting the renewed mind—utterly infuriating. Still, I love him for training me.

Our love for God is the main thing which did keep, and still keeps, us going. And a sense of humour is essential if we are to press on in this war. Sometimes it is either weep or laugh—and we choose to laugh. It's encouraging to those whose temperaments torment them that God *can* change us. Before I was baptised in the Spirit I was known as a misery, rarely seen to smile. The elders of the church in which I grew up used to have special prayer meetings in which they would ask God if he could somehow make Alex Buchanan happy. In time, God answered that prayer, and I do now laugh sometimes! Humour seems to have infected the whole family, too, so we praise God for fun. Our children were and still are such a joy to us.

Thank God that he is so ambitious for us. Thank God that his perspective is eternal, not transient. Small wonder that his answer to our cry 'Lord, please take us out of the arena' is simply and lovingly *'Why?'* Let those who are sick and frustrated take heart; there is hope with God. He can change our attitude. We must let him do it now!

In fact the time in Chester was fairly happy for

Peggy, despite the slow, continued deterioration in her condition. It was also happy for me at times. With the aid of her electric buggy Peggy was able to go out and visit people, shop, run our home, entertain, and live a comparatively normal life. An added joy was when she came with me to minister both in this country and abroad. In one year we went abroad eight times, as well as ministering all over the UK. Three of those trips were to Israel. Peggy loves travelling; and, during this time, she was able to keep MS very much in the background, with the belief that God would heal completely one day.

Perhaps the worst battle for Peggy's mind came next. God had blessed her work at Spring Harvest more than usual. She was so busy that I had to go at midnight and haul her away from people to whom she was still ministering! But then the trauma of moving, together with the shock of suddenly losing the use of her legs, suddenly hit her. When we had first looked over the house in York she was able to walk round it, albeit with sticks. Within three weeks she was in a wheelchair. This left her reeling for a while, and despondent. Surely God was a healing God! She began to believe that she must be in the last stages of MS. So the assault on our minds continued. Somehow, however, we did find grace from God to persevere in our arena.

9

Withdrawing to Get Closer

In acceptance lieth peace,
O my heart be still;
Let thy restless worries cease
And accept his will.
Though this test be not thy choice,
It is his—therefore rejoice.

In his plan there cannot be
Aught to make thee sad;
If this is his choice for thee,
Take it and be glad.
Make from it some lovely thing
To the glory of thy King.

Cease from sighs and murmuring,
Sing his loving grace,
This thing means thy furthering
To a wealthy place.
From thy fears he'll give release,
In acceptance lieth peace.

Hannah Hurnard

We enjoyed living in the lovely city of Chester, but we
had become rather weary of praying for healing. We

preferred now to spend more time praying for others, instead. A dear Christian osteopath helped us greatly with her skills and her prayers; we bless God for Christina Parsons. Despite her help, after our annual rigorous three-week stint at Spring Harvest, Peggy quite suddenly lost more of her mobility. She underwent yet more tests in hospital, but these only confirmed what we knew already: there was no prospect, humanly speaking, of any improvement at all.

Then some of the people in one of the two local churches we had attended felt that 'soaking prayer' was the answer. At the instigation of our eldest son Mark, they began a chain of prayer for her. They came to our home whenever they could to pray. Some encouraging words came and renewed our hope again. Several folk felt that we were up against a spirit of infirmity, so we began to pray for the destruction of this evil influence. I am not one of those who see demons everywhere, knowing that they are neither omnipresent, nor all-powerful, though they are real and active. So we prayed accordingly. As we did so, God gave me a simple word in my heart saying, 'It is time to take the gloves off.'

Gloves off

This new commitment to 'extraordinary prayer' required even more diligence in our personal life, so I stepped up my lifelong habit of prayer walks. I would walk for miles along the canal bank, and anywhere else I could find, in order to wage stronger warfare against the wicked one, and to besiege the throne of God about our health. Peggy too, as she drove her electric buggy to and through the city, stepped up her own prayers.

A fresh commitment also meant a more stringent review of my attitude to material things. God highlighted my apparently innocent habit of hoarding wood and screws! For many years we had had to make do and mend our various houses; hoarded wood had saved us a lot of money. However, in a time of intense conflict, we cannot be absorbed with things such as DIY. My years were running out fast; time was not on my side. Habits had to change.

God had dealt strongly with me before about things that distract. Once when I was a motor mechanic I had started to build my own car (registered as a Buchanan Special). At the same time, we were building the new church at Ruislip to which I have referred earlier. There came a moment when I had to decide which was most important: building the car, or getting on with the church. I do not pretend to have made a quick decision then, but I did decide after a while that the church came first.

Again, just before a prayer and Bible week, my car broke down. Having a wife and three children to transport 350 miles to the conference, I got bothered because I could not make it work. Everything else went by the board as I struggled with that wretched Cortina—including my prayer and preparation time! Suddenly, God spoke to me about my inordinate interest in that car, and about my love of machinery. He asked me to lay down love of cars for his sake. I had a struggle, but I did it, and have never worked on my cars since. As soon as I had given up my passion for cars, praying a prayer of surrender, the Cortina started straightaway!

Hobbies, and recreations of any sort are not wrong, but they must never get in the way of extending the kingdom of God. Sometimes God asks us to surrender them, but sometimes he gives them back to us.

What is the wilderness?

God drew us many times into the wilderness, so that we could be closer to him. When I use this term I mean a period of time during which the intensity of work, travel, and activity diminish. A time when God clearly indicates that he wants us in a quieter mode. He causes us to disentangle ourselves from the usual round, and even from much contact with people, so that we concentrate primarily on him and his word. We do not retreat from the world, but we use the best of our energies to concentrate on him. Times of illness can be such wilderness times—not that I believe God causes sickness, but I am sure he uses it to draw us nearer to him.

For many years I have struggled with the pain and embarrassment of it, especially on public platforms. It is sometimes difficult and even painful to enunciate words clearly; in fact, in earlier days the very words I wanted to come out strong and significant came out as refined raspberries, much to my chagrin. Those who have a visible handicap have to struggle with the feeling that their disability is so obvious that the minds of the congregation are fixed on their appearance, rather than the subject of their preaching. One of the men on the Spring Harvest platform in 1988 was a great help in this context. 'Alex, it is Christ I see in you,' he said. 'That is what grips me—not the shape of your face.' His comment was the grace of God to me.

There was even more evidence of the grace of God for me later on. When Spring Harvest had set up an internal TV network on the camp, I was asked to appear on the morning programme. They put the cameras on my 'wrong' side, but before I could ask them to swap them for my 'right' side, the interview started. I felt waves of embarrassment, but found grace to go on.

Later in the day a man came over and hugged me and hugged me. He said, 'Brother, you don't know what you have done for us; you just don't know what you have done.' I said, 'Quite right, brother, I don't know what I have done. What have I done?'

He told me this story. He and his wife were in their chalet watching the TV from the camp studio. His wife was sitting in utter depression and bitterness, because she had suffered from Bell's palsy for years. She had withdrawn into her shell, refusing to see anyone, and was slowly losing her faith in God. Suddenly she saw my battered face on the screen and began to listen to what I was saying about the courage of God in using the weak and foolish of the earth. She jumped to her feet saying, 'If God can use him, then he can use me.' At the same time she was overwhelmed by the Spirit's power. To quote her husband, their 'life began again'. Isn't God good?

God has courage enough to use any and every circumstance to get us apart with him in the wilderness. When Jesus was on earth, he said to his disciples, 'Come away by yourselves to a lonely place and rest awhile' (Mk 6:31). I sometimes interpret it this way: 'Come apart and rest awhile—or just come apart'!

In our work and warfare for God in this world, we are sometimes right in the front line and at other times further back. It is not a question of failure when God draws us back a bit; it is usually due to his understanding of us. He knows that we need to renew our resources, and to review our progress. In addition, we sometimes need to change our strategy. But over and above all, God wants us in a quieter place to speak more clearly to us, and to conform us even more to the image of his dear Son. All these purposes can be accomplished when he takes us into the wilderness.

The wilderness is not a place where God punishes his people for being naughty. It may be a place of correction (chastening), but he corrects because he loves, not because he delights in hurting us. Nor is it a place of banishment from his presence. It may not be easy to sense that he is with us there, but—as he promised in Hebrews 13:5—'I will never desert you, nor will I ever forsake you.' We may not be able actually to touch him, but he is with us. He has said so.

The wilderness is a place of reassessment, where priorities can be examined. It can be a place where, in the words of the old chorus, 'The things of earth can grow strangely dim, in the light of his glory and grace.' There, undistracted, we can see him in his glory, becoming more sensitive to his heart's desires. A place where true perspective is given, and the differences between working *with* God, and working *for* him is seen more clearly. After such experiences, we are less likely to relapse into ordinary Christianity. (By this I mean a Christian life in which we just attend services mechanically, read the Scriptures cursorily, pray desultorily, and experience little if any of God's power.)

The Christian life was never meant to be ordinary. God is not ordinary, so how can his people be ordinary? Our calling is a high calling. It is meant to be characterised by successful warfare, life-changing witness, prayer which changes nations, rejoicing in tribulation. The average Christian will not experience all these things all the time, for we all fail on occasion, and of course God uses us in the smaller things of life too, not always in the more spectacular. But we should look for and expect the extraordinary manifestations of his power in our life and be healthily dissatisfied with anything less.

Our Enemy is of course out to deflect us from such a life. One of his devices is the 'wearing out of the saints' mentioned in Daniel 7:25. We have experienced this more than once. For example, the building of the new church in Ruislip had made huge demands on our time, money, energy, and prayer life. For a long time we met those demands, but there came a time when we were worn out and began to lapse into the ordinary. Prayer became mechanical and muted, worship dull, the meetings formal; and we went back to our previous way of life: the ordinary. Then, in his mercy, God caused us to stop most of our activities for a while in order to refresh our hearts by deeper communion with him. We began to pray to him as part of our fellowship with him, instead of presenting him with a list of vital materials for the building. We began to read and teach the Scriptures as part of our feeding on God rather than just seeking new instructions about the building. It was not easy, for we were geared up for activity, but that change was necessary for our spiritual welfare. (We saw the fruit of it later when God wonderfully worked through the fellowship there, saved many, and built up their faith.) If we neglect the times of quiet, or wilderness, we do not achieve the purposes of God. What is the point of a new church if its members are spiritually worn out?

A similar thing had also happened in the building

of the new Assembly in Matlock. God had been
wonderfully at work at one time, but when unusual
prayer degenerated into ordinary prayer, worship
became formal, and we lowered our spiritual
sights—only concerned with getting the building
open—then God was no longer at liberty to work in
power. Therefore, although the building went up,
the spiritual life of the members languished. Again,
God in his mercy spoke clearly and strongly to us
about the need to go apart with him. There was a
good response which enabled God to make the
Assembly there one of the best and most fruitful
churches in the whole area.

Danger of decline

Most of us start well in our walk with God and in our
service for him, but in many cases the rigours of such
a life take their toll, and we withdraw into a rather
mechanical Christianity in which we go through the
motions rather than work with God in vibrant life.
Most of us then need a time in the wilderness where
we meet God again, and where our priorities are
re-established.

Preaching the Scriptures can be a thrilling
occupation, and even the demands of preparation
can be a joy, until the anointing diminishes, or until
we begin to tire. Then it is all too easy to lapse into the
easier mechanical preparation and delivery; in other
words, into the ordinary.

In Ruislip my preaching was not too thrilling
initially, either to me, or to the long-suffering congregation. My first sermon was a shock to everyone. I
started with 1 Corinthians: 1:30; 'By his doing you
are in Christ Jesus, who became to us wisdom from
God, and righteousness, and sanctification, and

redemption.' After floundering around for twenty-five minutes, I ended up by using the verse as a ringing denunciation of the theory of evolution! One elder's wife, who had recovered more quickly than the elders, comforted me by saying, 'Alex, you chose some lovely hymns.' Years later when God began to anoint me to preach with his power, and I enjoyed it, there were results. But when the power diminished and results were scanty, I fell back into the ordinary, and the people knew it.

Evangelism is an exciting, albeit demanding ministry, and there is no other joy like that of winning souls. In Jubilee Chapel in Liverpool we had kept a record of 140 people who were born again during our years there. It was great to see young and old come to the Saviour, but when we were exhausted and conversions became rare, it was as easy to retreat into the ordinary in Liverpool as in Ruislip and simply conduct a holy huddle every Sunday.

Like most Christians, Peggy and I have pressed on and rejoiced most of the time, but there have been times when the effort has been too much. At these times the cost of ministry has seemed too steep, and New Testament Christianity has been too demanding. So on these occasions I at least have settled for less. But in his faithfulness, God has always taken a hand by leading us back into the quiet place, and there he has renewed us time after time. That is why we still have a ministry today.

'Subtle love of softening things'

This quotation from Amy Carmichael's writings in *Gold Cord* began to convict me during our time in Chester. I realised at one stage that we had no engagements booked for two weeks, and that I could therefore rearrange the garden, a boring oblong of land behind our bungalow. Then, reading the *TV Times*, I saw a whole list of good programmes coming up. In addition, I was tempted to fit some extra instruments to our car. Now none of these things was wrong in itself, but I had a secret desire to slow down in Christian work; to pull back from its rigours; to lower my sights; to give way to 'the subtle love of softening things'. To settle for smaller ambitions is a temptation that comes to us all at times, and I confess that for a while my ambition was to stay at home and grow roses.

One reason for this was that in my perspective God had become too small. I had lost my early vision of him, and my disappointment over the lack of power in my ministry had clouded my spirit; I was ready to settle for less if it took away the heavy responsibility of sustaining a demanding ministry. This has happened to me more than once, although Peggy has not given way to the same extent. At such times gloom has set in, and the joy of the Lord has been displaced. However, although I have to testify to the times of gloom and failure, I can also testify to the many many times when God has lifted me up and restored my soul. His treatment has sometimes been drastic, but it has always been restorative. He has restored both spiritual health, and vital ministry.

Christian life has seasons

Life goes in seasons: seasons of trial, of success, of failure; and most seasons consist either of learning, unlearning, or relearning. There seems no end to this process, but instead of being depressed about that, it is better to see all our circumstances as opportunities.

In one of my first Bibles I wrote this: 'Our daily trials are God-given opportunities to decide between God's will and our own.' Some years later I also wrote: 'There are three things which never return: the sped arrow, the spoken word, and a lost opportunity.' If we use the opportunities which circumstances present, then we lay up treasure in heaven; but if we lose them or rather refuse them, we are that much poorer in heaven. We have to choose!

Our Enemy would love us to settle for less than God's best, and our own wicked hearts would often co-operate with him. But thank God for the courageous Holy Spirit who outwits the Enemy. He continually sets before us the goals of God, and urges us on to reach them. May God grant us to see the value of opportunities, and the grace to take them.

God used our time in Chester to raise our faith, to change our outlook, and our priorities, despite all the traumatic things I have written about here. So again we say, 'Thank God for the wilderness.' God drew us back to get closer.

10

Narrowing the Focus for Greater Vision

It is quite frightening to realise that one is on the last lap of active work in the kingdom. Suddenly what Peggy and I used to call our thirty-five-year plan (when decorating or gardening, etc) now has to be called our ten-year plan! The thought that in a few years' time we might be in glory is alternately thrilling and frightening; thrilling, because we will be with the Father we love; and frightening, because time and energy suddenly seem so short. However, all is well if we tackle things properly. So we began to reassess our life.

Focus on a home

First we needed a new spiritual home. Not many churches are able to cope with those to whom God has given a strong or 'awkward' ministry. But those with such a gifting greatly need love; they need to be accountable to other strong and godly men, and to be backed up in their ministry. Feeling the need to be enfolded in such a strong fellowship, we prayed deeply and looked around for it.

God had brought us into renewed fellowship with some good friends in York whom we had known when we lived there before. These, including Ross and Christine Paterson, together with others, had formed the Acomb Christian Fellowship. It was founded in prayer, and was known for its intercessory life. The Acomb Christians joined with us in prayer for our situation, and this, as well as the love and prayer from the Chester folk, encouraged us greatly to press on. Another helpful thing was to attend Acomb's men's prayer and fasting weekends. They helped restore the prophetic revelation without which ministry like mine is virtually useless. They also served to remind me that intercession is heavily dependent on revelation.

As our fellowship with Acomb developed, we had an increasing desire to join them. We talked long and honestly with the elders; and after explaining the peculiar nature of some of our work, making it plain that we were not looking for finance, position, or featherbedding, but simply a base and a home, they welcomed us gladly. So in September 1987 we moved to York.

It was not a trouble-free move. Moving house comes quite high on anyone's stress scale, and we were no exceptions. Our lovely 'saleable' bungalow just did not sell. We wondered whether God was restraining us, or the devil hindering us. With hindsight we can see now that the critical thing was the timing. Our present and infinitely suitable house in York was not available till later on. Thank God he kept it for us!

For me, the move to York was a mixture of

challenge and anxiety. For Peggy it was a difficult time: a new home, adjusting to the continuous use of a wheelchair indoors and out, as well as the sadness of the death of her mother. Those traumas have certainly cast Peggy more on the Lord. The chorus 'The Lord knows the way through the wilderness' became particularly meaningful to her, and she sought to cling to that truth. The doctor had prescribed tablets to relax her muscles, because her knees had become fixed in a sitting position, but these tablets are quite indiscriminate in their effects. They relaxed nearly everything. She began to sleep like a log, and consequently developed a painful pressure sore. She therefore immediately stopped taking the tablets, and for several months was awake most of the night. She would get up to read her Bible, or books about healing or faith. She would do the ironing, make cakes—do anything to get tired or pass the time. She also developed a morbid attitude, again thinking she must be in the last stages of MS, and wondering if God wanted to take her home to heaven so that she would not hinder my ministry. Because she did not want to fight against God's will, she was very puzzled. Was she resisting God, or not? Where did all this pain and heartache and deep disappointment fit with God's promise of healing? We both desired healing, but where were we in our search? Was it God's move next, or ours?

To be honest, I felt that God did not seem to do much to help her. Her faith was sorely tried, and so was mine! I felt utterly helpless, a complete fraud. Despite all my preaching, I could not help my own dear wife.

Focus on the ministry

It is all too easy to spend our time doing what I call
uncommanded work. It may seem to produce fruit,
but did God give us that work to do, or were we
pressured into it by men, or even our own unsancti-
fied ambition? Uncommanded work brings no
reward at the judgement seat of Christ. Periodic
review is therefore important.

The diminishing abilities of later years mean that
we must find out where to use our time, energy and
gifting to the best advantage. Like many of God's
servants, Peggy and I have several giftings. This is not
boasting; it is simply a recognition of what God has
been pleased to do for us. God showed us these gifts
through some godly friends. For example, I had a
major pastoral ministry; something of a teaching gift;
some ability in administration; and a clear prophetic
gift. Peggy has an administrative gift; a pastoral heart
which enables her to counsel in depth; a growing
ability to prophesy; and authority in prayer.

In York, particularly for me, it was time to distinguish the major gifts from the minor, the useful
from the vital, still avoiding the danger of becoming a
specialist. Over-emphasis on any doctrine or avenue
of service can lead to pride or tunnel vision. So we
rarely go to preach in a church on a 'one-off' basis,
nor do we respond to many invitations to small
gatherings. It is not that we despise them; in fact,
much of our ministry in the past has been to small
and struggling churches. But our watchword nowadays is economy: of time, energy, and gifting. We ask
God to show us those events which will yield the best
results for him.

Our counselling is more selective, and our teaching
is mainly done in those conferences which give us the

greatest opportunities among the greatest number of people. This has nothing to do with aiming for the highest financial return, for this has never ever been our motive. Nor should it be.

I have never reckoned myself a great preacher, or a 'signs and wonders' type, but I know that the prophetic ministry is the strongest gift God has given to me, and now I could see that it was time to exercise it to a greater degree. We reviewed together those times when God would give me many clear and powerful visions, words of knowledge, and clear understanding of where people (especially church leaders) and churches were in their careers. This prophetic ministry was usually, though not exclusively, done quietly. It most often occurred after good friendship was established, although there were some occasions when God sent me to people I had never met. In York, feeling that this aspect of my work had somewhat diminished, we resolved that it was time to concentrate on it again, even if we had to curtail other things for which we were gifted by God.

Focus on the churches

It is both joyful and awful to see a church's condition from God's perspective: wonderful to see the sincere love, and the godly activity in so many of them, but awful to see the hypocrisy and secret sin in others. Tears are a real part of the prophetic ministry, frustration a constant companion. Vision has a cost, and I for one do not easily pay it. Of all the ministries, the prophetic is one of the most painful, and it is certainly not the one I would have chosen. It needs great grace, and some grit, and it has some flashes of glory!

Several times as I preached in various churches, I
noticed with alarm the drained condition of the
pastor. Through the prophetic word God has shown
that if they did not stop for a while, then they would
either die or have a breakdown. Praise God, most
listened and were delivered from premature 'pro-
motion'.

Other experiences were not so good. In one church
God revealed adultery in the life of an elder, and
addiction to pornography in one of the deacons.
They refused to repent, rejecting the word from God.
God then said through further prophecy that he had
written 'the glory has departed' above the church; it
closed down some time afterwards. One another
occasion God revealed that a serious quarrel had been
festering between two of the main leaders for a long
time. The resulting dryness in the church had all but
killed its life; but as I appealed to the leaders to end
their strife, God broke in, and the people began to cry
out to God to restore the blessing. One of the
quarrelling leaders openly repented of his bitterness,
reaching out to the other man, but he would not be
reconciled. Through a further prophecy God warned
him of the outcome, but he still refused to respond.
He died ten days later. The prophecy did not kill
him; it simply brought things to a head in his life,
giving him the chance to repent. But he did not do it,
and so God's word to him was fulfilled.

I found that the chief enemies of a prophet are
church leaders with a power complex. Such men are
scared of being unmasked as empire builders, and
they find subtle ways either of watering down the
prophetic word brought to their church, or of deni-
grating the reputation of the prophet. Some hear the
word and accept that it is from God; but because it

cuts across their plans, they bury it. My sadness so
often was to see the consequences of their action as
the church either diminished or replaced living
witness with mere activity. Further pain came because
in some cases the fulfilment of the word was delayed.
Then power-hungry leaders took the opportunity to
cry 'false prophet'. I know of no greater pain than
that of feeling that I had missed the mind of God and
prophesied falsely in his name. God rarely allows a
prophet to justify himself and often leaves him
apparently stranded, at the mercy of those who long
to destroy him.

At such times I often felt a strong urge to stick to
prophecies that would be approved and commended
by men. I know it is sinful merely to be men-pleasers,
but I confess I was tempted to take that path. I looked
earnestly for men who would understand my
situation and come to my rescue, but I found few.
Then God put this question in my heart: 'Which do
you want most? The approval of men, or the privilege
of being my messenger, whatever the cost?' At first I
answered glibly, 'O Lord, I do want the privilege of
being your servant.' But on reflection, I found that
the approval of men still loomed large in my mind. I
wanted to be accepted and liked. There followed yet
more repentance, and God performed more heart
surgery.

Further afield

As well as prophesying in churches, God caused me to
prophesy in other places—public places, too! I found
it daunting to approach total strangers with the
prophetic word, especially when it revealed their past
or present crises. Yet it was a privilege. Broken
ministers were restored in a short time as God showed

them not only their condition, but what he was willing and able to do about it. Broken marriages were mended; lifelong feuds were resolved; churches were reoriented. These were some of the pleasant aspects of the ministry. Others, not so pleasant, involved the closing of churches, the departure of leaders from the ministry, and so on.

Once I was waiting in the lobby of an hotel when I saw a man in a bright blue suit standing alone. I assumed from his bright blue suit that he was an American! As I looked at him, God urged me to go over to him. Being a coward, I hesitated; but, sensing that there was tragedy in this man's life, I went over to him. He looked at me but said nothing. Eventually I plucked up courage and said to him, 'There is no need for your marriage to break up, and you don't need to cut your throat with the knife which you have in your pocket, because God will help you.'

He and I were both rather surprised by this; then his eyes opened wide, and he turned to me with his fists clenched. I waited for the knockout, but it never came. Instead, he flung his arms round me and wept and wept, rather to my embarrassment. It emerged that he was a Canadian minister who had ruined his marriage by getting immersed in his work and forgetting his own wife's need of pastoral care. He had also neglected his relationship with God. His church had declined as a result. He had no one to pastor him, so he had concluded that life was hopeless. He had come to see an old friend for the last time, and then planned to kill himself with the razor in his pocket. Mercifully, God saved him.

On another occasion I had to warn a preacher by giving a prophecy which said that if he went on his projected preaching tour he would die in the middle of it. He listened, went to his doctor (who confirmed that he would have died), and took the sabbatical that saved his life and ministry.

As well as those personal and church prophecies, God gave me revelations about Britain. Some of these national prophecies, mentioned in my book *Bible Meditation, Prayer and Prophecy* were given during the time when Denis Clark and I worked together, and they came with increasing frequency as I spoke in churches of all denominations. I still cherish the hope that some will rise up and act in the light of those prophecies.

So many such events could be recorded, though not all as dramatic, but it is not wise for me to write more here. I have no desire for a name or reputation. The important thing is not that God uses Alex Buchanan (as well as many many others) in this way, but that we take notice of what God says to his church through the various ministries which he has given to it.

Focus on the war

We have found that one prerequisite for total engagement in spiritual warfare is a holy hatred of sin and of the Enemy. Mere dislike is not enough. Hebrews 1:9 does not say Jesus disliked sin, but that he *HATED* it. Why are we so tolerant when God is not? 'Holy hatred' does not mean that we roar out imprecatory prayers in the prayer meetings, nor should we glare malevolently at sinners. We are not talking about the human malicious kind of hatred here! However, unless we realise what awful damage is being done to God's fair creation, we will never wage that war in which no mercy is asked or given.

Intercession requires revelation

In order to discover the Enemy's strategy, and then to combat it with the strategy of God, it is vital to see what is going on in the heavenly places. In one of the Intercessors International gatherings in Belfast, I recall a clear vision of a black throne, with an evil prince sitting on it. The throne was positioned right above the city, and hordes of demons were engaged in fostering all the ancient hatreds, rumours, and lies by which this Enemy has retained his hold over the land, just as other powers do in the rest of Britain. We had been floundering in prayer and needed some insight. When God gave this vision we were able to pray with greater vigour, and we did so. I saw a leg of the throne begin to crack, and the evil prince showed some fear. The lesser powers began to run, and then great, good angels appeared on the scene in large numbers, enforcing the power of God in response to our intercessions. There is no magic ending to this, for the conflict in Ireland rages to this day, but the memory of it stirs me afresh to feel my way back to an even greater involvement in the conflict which will go on until the great Day dawns and Jesus returns in all his glory.

Narrowing our focus for greater or clearer vision enables us to wage the warfare of God far more effectively. Paul said in 1 Corinthians 9:26: 'I box [fight] in such a way, not beating the air.' In other words, he clearly saw the opponent, as well as the best way of hitting him, then got on with it.

If we really love the Lord, and his desires are embedded in our hearts, we cannot stay long out of his war. The sheer cost of it may cause us to retreat for a while, but eventually the shame of it, plus its measly returns, causes us to go back to God and to ask him for the grace to resume the war. When we do so, the Holy Spirit comes with great delight to show us our best giftings, then takes us by the hand, saying, 'I have been waiting for you. Now we can get on and fight effectively.' Peggy and I came to him, took his hand, and now we are 'bashing on'.

11

Persevering in Partnership

During our last years in Chester my thought had been that we were really heading for early retirement. Invitations to minister had diminished; Peggy's sickness and my increasing weariness precluded the frequent travel of former years during which we had often travelled 30,000 miles a year in the UK, as well as making several trips abroad. We needed a renewed vision, and even the will to go on.

These wilderness seasons do not last for ever, unless we are so unresponsive or obstinate that God has to leave us there. Peggy and I were not dis-obedient, so God did not leave us there, but drew us out of it into a new chapter of our life. I don't think God invented retirement, although I am sure he is not against the state pension!

'Man's extremity is God's opportunity'

I do not know who wrote the above phrase, but I do know that God loves to bring us to where we cry, 'Lord, to whom else can we go?' Getting us to a place

where we realise our utter dependence on God alone
is the aim of the Godhead. The Father desires it; the
Son showed in his life on earth that such dependence
was possible; the Spirit engineers it. He sometimes
does this by using the Enemy's desire to drive us to
despair; as Paul says, 'We are afflicted in every way,
but not crushed; perplexed, but not despairing; per-
secuted, but not forsaken; struck down, but not
destroyed' (2 Cor 4:8–9).

While the devil's strategy is intended to crush us, or
render us helpless in a wrong way, the Holy Spirit
sometimes uses these schemes of the Enemy to make
us helpless in a right way: ie, humanly helpless, but
therefore candidates for divine enabling.

A glimpse of a wrestling ring helped me in my
thinking about this. The goodie was being badly
beaten up by the bully; he was on the floor in his
corner, too battered to get up and rest for a minute.
Someone gave him a swig of something strong. He
heard some warm, encouraging words from his
helper. Then he got up and, fighting cleanly but
ruthlessly, threw the bully out of the ring and won the
contest.

Divine hatred

Having learned more about hating sin and hating the
Enemy, it was now time to be as ruthless with the
Enemy as he was with us. Before anyone can wrestle
with him, however, he must first be ruthless with his
own flesh. A life which is not surrendered to God is
surrendered to his Enemy. When you present
yourselves as slaves for obedience, you are slaves of
the one whom you obey, either of sin, resulting in
death, or of obedience resulting in righteousness
(Rom 6:16). A life which is surrendered to God

ensures victory in battle, since God is for the humble (surrendered). God is in our corner; God gives us a swig of something strong; God encourages us with a word, and out goes the Enemy. It is important that we give no quarter to the wicked one, for he certainly gives none to us.

Satan's hatred

A vivid reminder of the Enemy's hatred of us came during our first few months in York. For many years I had driven many thousands of miles; and in forty-three years of driving I had never had an accident. But on our removal journey to live in York we had an accident! We were not hurt, though quite shocked. There followed another uneventful period, when we were again travelling far. Then in October 1988 we were on our way to lead a school of prayer in a nearby town, when a van driver crossed the dual carriageway and stopped, leaving us nowhere to go except straight into him. Again, praise God, we were unhurt (as was the driver); no traffic came up behind us, praise God. But we were again quite shaken.

To cap it all, on our thirty-first wedding anniversary, we were trundling peacefully down a country lane when a car came speeding round a bend, straight into us. This time I was quite deeply shocked. Three accidents in less than eighteen months! I went away to seek God to find out what was going on, and he gave me a clear picture of the scene in the heavenly places.

I realised that thirty years of strong spiritual warfare such as those in the prayer and Bible weeks had made us dangerous enough to arouse the wrath of the Evil One; and that he was intent on killing us, or at least causing us to lose our nerve so that we would tone down our prayers and perhaps stop them altogether.

My beloved partner

Peggy has always been a dear helper to me, and to any who needed her. For years she has given loving counsel to the people who came to our home. But now, because of God's strong but gracious dealings with her, and her response to those dealings, she gives them counsel with an even more powerful anointing, one which has an even greater effect on those who come to her. Her godly reaction to her sufferings has enabled God to entrust a deeper ministry to her. God has especially helped her work with those who, like us, have had to deal with the frustration of not being healed as they press on with the extension of the kingdom. In her quiet way she ministers to many folk, not only Christians, but to the lost among the shoppers in the city. She is well known as the lady with the buggy, and the shop assistants love to talk to her.

She knows the valley of the shadow as well as anyone; she understands well the torment of knowing and loving Scripture, but living with it unfulfilled in her own particular circumstances. She has had to adapt from being a very active person to being largely crippled. Her times of anguish have been frequent, and despair has more than once brought her low. Yet through it all she has persevered more than anyone I know. Her courage and faithfulness surpasses that of most. If ever anyone has given God a demonstration of utter loving faithfulness by which he is glorified, she has.

I'll leave the next part of the book to her.

Peggy's story

It was a terrible shock to me when I lost the use of my legs. As Alex has already said, when we went to view the house we eventually bought in York, I was able to walk round it. But just before we moved in, I could not walk or stand at all. I felt so sad; I had already lost most of my young womanhood and the freedom that most young women enjoy. And now, just when the children were all married and away and Alex and I could be free to go more or less anywhere we wanted to, I could not walk at all. Liberty seemed even further away.

Many things went through my mind as we fell asleep on our first night in York. How could I keep this house tidy? How could I get in and out of it when Alex was away ministering? Is this to be a prison now more than a home? In fact it is a lovely home, and we are happy here. It is also very well adapted to our needs, also to those of the members of the leadership training programme we hold here. Still, in those first days, I wondered what we were doing in such a place.

God graciously led Ulla, one of the ladies from our fellowship, to come and help us in the house. She keeps it beautifully clean. Peter, one of the men, made ramps for the wheelchair so that I could get into the garden in my electric buggy. When I am out shopping in this vehicle, and I see women laden with heavy bags, it makes me grateful that I can shop so easily. Plastic bags dangle from my handlebars, and tins and boxes perch precariously on the back, but I manage! Others in the fellowship help me, such as Jean, who takes me often to osteopathy, and Reg, who does the same.

I am grateful to all these dear folk, and I am glad to be alive, grateful for God's grace on which I truly live, but it is still a daily struggle to get moving. It takes me quite a while to get dressed (who invented shoe laces?). Then I have to limber up the best I can before I try to do some work in the house. On a Monday I must go to physiotherapy at the hospital; then to osteopathy twenty miles away on a Tuesday; then to physio again on a Wednesday. Interspersed are trips to the hospital pool for therapeutic swimming. In addition, there are meals to get ready, and the administration of Cherith Trust. I still travel and minister with Alex, with all the preparation involved in that. But it is not all bad. Let me say again how grateful I am that I can still do so much, but I cannot say that I am completely satisfied; how can I be unless God shows me his great power in healing?

Although I long to be healed and am at present taking healing seriously, there are some advantages in being ill. One is that I have been able to talk to people about Jesus and his love, goodness and care; people do listen carefully. When I talk about the ways in which he has helped me, they know I am not talking rubbish. I have had lovely opportunities to share the gospel with many kinds of people.

Many people stop to talk to me about my buggy. Many of these folk notice the stickers I have put on the back; one reads 'My other car is a Porsche', and the others says 'Buckingham Palace Car Park'. They are useful for starting conversations, and I often hear people behind me reading the stickers and laughing. Sometimes this leads to a personal testimony or even a challenge to them. In fact I rarely go out without challenging somebody about the Lord Jesus. Disability can cause embarrassment, but humour helps to counter this. The disabled must make it easy for those who are well to talk with them and feel at ease when they do.

One day in Chester when I stopped outside a shop, a woman came up to me, leaned on the arm of the buggy and said, 'I'm exhausted, but that sticker has made my day.' The manager of Boots in Chester would say, 'I'm glad you've not brought your Porsche today.' Often I would be approached by people asking if I thought such a buggy would suit their disabled relative. The stickers show people that I am human and approachable.

Sadly, it is easy, though understandable, for disabled people to become absorbed with their disability. We who are disabled live continually with our aches, pains, and frustrations, so that our thinking almost necessarily revolves around ourselves. I say 'almost' because these things do not need to consume us. I could give Alex a daily report on my illness; this pain, or that funny feeling, or these spasms—and I have done sometimes. But complaining does not help either of us; rather, it brings us down. So I find it best not to give the pains and spasms much publicity. Occasionally it is good and necessary to have a sympathetic ear, and to pray together; this prevents me from falling into the habit of complaining. Chris, one of the young women from the fellowship, comes to pray with me for my healing as often as she can, and this is a great encouragement to me.

Those who are whole need to understand the feelings of the disabled, and to be careful over them without 'smothering' them. Once, at a conference, Alex and I were talking with a group of people. Someone then came hovering, wanting to talk to him. One friend suddenly said, 'Alex, I will take Peggy so that you can talk to this person.' I was saddened by her sheer thoughtlessness. When we want to help the disabled, a useful thing is to ask them if they want to be helped, or if they would rather be left alone. In that way the disabled feel more in control of their situation, and we avoid humiliating them.

Alex is partly deaf, and has in the past been most embarrassed by people who back him against a wall, shouting loudly at him to make him hear. The thing to do is to face him (or anyone who is partly deaf), speak clearly but not in an exaggerated fashion—then, of course, refrain from putting a hand in front of the mouth. A moustache is an enemy of lip reading; brightly coloured lipstick is a friend. Take your pick, depending on gender!

Christians should far more than others be careful in their treatment of the disabled. For example, avoid walking just in front of the wheelchair when talking to them; then they won't have to concentrate on avoiding your feet! Avoid trapping them in long-winded conversation; they may want the loo! When you pass through swing doors, look behind to see if there is a wheelchair about to follow; it saves flattened toes. And so on. Have fun thinking of situations that demand extra care!

We live in an age of protests and fights for rights. As a disabled person I feel that we or our carers should indeed approach civic bodies and government departments to present our particular needs and problems. We should present cogent arguments in a Christlike manner, but I am saddened when I see this done in a way that uses the arguments as weapons or put in an aggressive way. In the Bible James and John wanted to call down fire on those who opposed Jesus, but that did not honour the Lord, nor would it today. A soft answer does 'turn away wrath'. Persistence is commendable, but the needs of the disabled must not become a battering ram hewed by the frustration of the disabled, or their carers.

The relationship between the sufferer and the carer is epitomised by the 'does he take sugar?' syndrome. A good carer (parent, husband, wife, or friend) would say 'Ask him.' The relationship is one of interdependent dignity. And, as the Bible says 'by love serve one another'. A carer is not a slave at the beck and call of the sufferer, nor is the latter a child to be bossed about for his or her own 'good'.

I like to think I am no trouble at all, but the truth is that although I may not be a trouble, I am a consideration. When Alex and I go away on ministry trips, he has to fold the wheelchair and lift it into the boot every time, and then get it out and let me get into it when we arrive. This is not an earth-shattering responsibility, but it is yet one more demand on him. We have both had to adjust to this way of life, and it is not easy.

Sometimes I have been guilty of seeking healing rather than the Healer, but God has shown me that healing is not a commodity. I believe Jesus died for our sicknesses as well as our sins. He himself took our infirmities and carried away our diseases (Mt 8:17). I want all he has done for me in the Atonement; it cost Jesus everything he had to die for me, and I don't want to miss anything at all. Having said that, he is my Lord and King, so I cannot *demand* anything from him as my right. But I do not want to miss anything through lack of searching.

There are many mysteries; we all know godly people who have not been healed. I do not know why, but that does not stop me from seeking Jesus about my own healing. I believe God can heal; I believe that he has healed people. In fact I know two people who have been healed of MS. This encourages me, but when God gives me faith I shall know deep in my

spirit that it is time to heal me. I will not just think, I
will know. So far this is not true of me but all is not
lost. Faith comes by hearing and hearing by the word
of God (Rom 10:17). This does not just mean listening to a Bible verse; it means the kind of hearing
that is mixed with God-given faith. This is what I look
and wait for, *expectantly*!

I still wrestle with some things. For example, I take
quite a few vitamin supplements. Sometimes I
wonder if that is trying to heal myself because of an
independent or fearing spirit—or is it co-operating
with God? Should I give them up as an act of faith?
Yet they actually do help me, for I have noticed the
difference when I have stopped taking some of them.

I struggle also with sadness when some 'anniver-
saries' come. I remember that on a particular day, a
year ago, or five years ago, I could still walk, or I
could still do this or that. Old photographs torment
me, when I see that I did not use a stick then, or I
could run about with the children. Nor can I be the
grandma I would love to be, because I am dependent
on others for transport, and our daughter and son-in-
law live 250 miles away. However, when I do get to
Andover, Alexandra, our granddaughter, loves to
push me around in my wheelchair because she is
about the same height. She says, 'Grandma, I think
we will do this'—as she pushes me towards her
kitchen set, or whatever she wants to do at the time.
She loves me to read stories to her, and I love to do so.
But despite these good times, I have to hold Father's
hand tightly indeed during the others.

Alex resumes

As I write, we are very busy, and nowhere near any
condition resembling retirement.

Among our varied activities nowadays, many of which we run under the umbrella of our own small private trust (Cherith Trust), is the Northern Links Fellowship, which helps to unite and serve churches and leaders in the North of England. I lead this, with the help of Ross Paterson, Harry Hughes and David Stephens. We also run a leadership training programme with them. It is such a joy to work with them in the important task of helping leaders into better leadership. Peggy and I are among the pastors to the Spring Harvest Team; I am an elder at large of the Acomb Christian Fellowship; and we keep in touch with many churches and their leaders to encourage them and offer a shoulder to cry on sometimes. All this keeps us both well occupied—far from bored, or retired!

The biggest problem is to make time to be alone with God so that when people do come for help, we bring them the relevant, living *rhema* (word) from God. I cannot claim that we always do so, but we certainly try. The Christian world is full of advice, but it is woefully short of divine counsel.

As for our healing, we are spending more time thanking God by faith for our healing than we are asking for it. We are in good heart, but still unsatisfied. We were hoping to add a final chapter testifying to God's healing, and thus giving him glory, but perhaps the 'glory' part of this book's title will come as people see us coping with the frustration of not being healed, yet still getting on with the ministry. Our motto is still 'Thou shalt bash on'. So we do.

Afterword from Our Children

Our children were very keen to add a few comments to this book, so let us introduce them.

Ruth, our firstborn, bore the brunt of our initial parenting, and like all firstborn children she suffered from our blunders and inexperience; however, she does not seem to have been marred for life! She became a Christian quite early on, and grew into a faithful and thoughtful disciple of Jesus. Being thoughtful has its problems, and she, more than the boys, understood the difficulties of having sick parents.

Mark, our eldest son, became a true Christian when he was three years old, and has never gone back on his decision. He has worked in industry, and in full-time Christian work. He has the budding ministry of a prophet, and has endured the rigours of the tough training necessary for that.

Andrew, our youngest son, was saved quite early on as we travelled in the car on the M1. He is the entrepreneur of the family and very successful in business. He has a winsome way with people, and God

uses him to speak to them of Jesus. He also has a great
ministry among young people.

Here are their comments.

Ruth

I believe that Mum and Dad would have had a
ministry even if they had not been ill, but I am sure
that their sickness has enhanced it. Mum, because she
was not able to dash around, is more available for
people to come and talk to her. She has had to learn
to take things more slowly, and this has made her
even more attentive to others and their needs. Her
cheerful nature has undoubtedly inspired and
encouraged others; and the fact that she never
complains despite her pain, discomfort, and frustration is a great witness to many. Dad's coping for
many years with deafness, pain, and frustration is a
testimony to the Lord's enabling grace. The way in
which they have coped with their troubles has been a
strong witness to many, many people, encouraging so
many to 'bash on', as Dad always says. This can only
be good. One of the best things to me is that in heaven
Mum's and Dad's rewards will be truly great, and this
thrills me as much as anything.

Mark

Our parents' reactions to their problems showed us
that there is more to life than perfect health. I marvel
at the great quality of their ministry. Their selfless-
ness has put the sort of edge on their service which is
comparatively rare. Their outstanding humility,
unselfishness, and godliness has brought great benefit
to thousands of people. The price was high, but they

paid it; the pressure was immense, but they stood up to it. An aura of respect follows them everywhere, and this glorifies God, which is precisely what they both want. Thank God for them.

Andrew

Dad was always my mentor on spiritual things; he would speak very clearly, but always with grace. He has a close relationship with God, with clearly defined objectives in his spiritual life. As I grew older he became my friend as well as my father and mentor.

Mum was always 'my dear mum'; I could talk to her about anything and at any time (usually around midnight). Mum's character was just as strong as Dad's; she persevered all the time, and is a great and godly woman. Peggy Buchanan has MS, but MS does not have Peggy Buchanan. Without my parents' love, teaching and example, I doubt if I would ever have found Jesus as my Saviour; I thank God for them, and for my Saviour.

Awaiting The Healer

by Margie Willers

Margie Willers travelled 10,000 miles for a miracle. But God did not answer her prayer.

Born with cerebral palsy, Margie stuggled through enormous difficulties—and even rejection—with amazing grit and humour. While others were miraculously healed of illnesses and disabilities, Margie was to find faith for a different kind of healing.

Her story tells how God is with her in the intense heat of her pain, anger and despair, miraculously binging a healing of heart and a rare depth of trust. Now, from her wheelchair, Margie brings the love of Christ to thousands of disabled people, awakening the church to their needs and potential.

'Margie is frequently being told that if only she had more faith she would be healed. I can tell you from experience that it takes infinitely more faith to go on serving and loving God in a wheelchair than ever it takes to walk away from one.'

—JENNIFER REES LARCOMBE

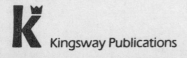

Kingsway Publications